negotiations

What the best negotiators know, do and say

second edition

Nic Peeling

Prentice Hall
is an imprint of

PEARSON

Harlow, England • London • New York • Boston • San Francisco • Toronto • Sydney • Singapore • Hong Kong
Tokyo • Seoul • Taipei • New Delhi • Cape Town • Madrid • Mexico City • Amsterdam • Munich • Paris • Milan

PEARSON EDUCATION LIMITED

Edinburgh Gate
Harlow CM20 2JE
Tel: +44 (0)1279 623623
Fax: +44 (0)1279 431059
Website: www.pearsoned.co.uk

First published in Great Britain in 2008
Second edition, 2011

Pearson Education is not responsible for the content of third party internet
sites.

ISBN: 978-0-273-74324-8

British Library Cataloguing-in-Publication Data
A catalogue record for this book is available from the British Library

Library of Congress Cataloging-in-Publication Data
Peeling, Nic.
   Brilliant negotiations : what the best negotiators know, do and say /
Nic Peeling. -- 2nd ed.
      p. cm.
   ISBN 978-0-273-74324-8 (pbk.)
1. Negotiation in business. I. Title.
   HD58.6.P43 2011
   658.4'052--dc22
                              2010040000

10 9 8 7 6 5 4 3 2 1
14 13 12 11 10

Cartoon illustrations by Bill Piggins
Typeset in 10/14pt Plantin Regular by 3
Printed and bound in Great Britain by Henry Ling Ltd, Dorchester, Dorset

To Arthur Williams

About the author

Nic Peeling had more than 15 years' experience as a front-line manager working for QinetiQ – a leading international defence and security technology company. Formerly an award-winning software researcher, he has a doctorate from the Computing Laboratory at Oxford University. Nic is now a Visiting Fellow at Cranfield University.

Nic remembers vividly all the mistakes he made in the process of becoming an experienced negotiator – experiences that have driven his interest in discovering and distilling what brilliant negotiators know, do and say.

Visit www.nicpeeling.com

Contents

Acknowledgements

I am indebted to my publisher Samantha Jackson for asking me to write this book and helping me to design and refine the content and structure. Thanks to Martina O'Sullivan for editing this second edition. Thanks also to Richard Stagg of Pearson Education for his insightful suggestions on the content. I am very grateful to the rest of the Pearson team for their great professionalism.

I was greatly helped by the wonderful input I got from my test readers: Chris Cant, Neil Hepworth, Barry Horne and Kay Hughes.

Introduction

Welcome to the second edition of *Brilliant Negotiations*. The first edition has stood the test of time very well indeed, but about 25 per cent of new material has been added. Two major new areas have been added. I have written a new chapter titled *How to become a brilliant negotiator*. This explains the techniques you can use to improve your negotiating skills, and having improved them how you can keep those skills honed. It will be useful for both complete novices and for those who already have some practical experience of negotiations. The second major addition builds on an aspect of *Brilliant Negotiations* that is unusual for a book on negotiations. Most negotiations books concentrate on the negotiations you will undertake in your job. *Brilliant Negotiations* also spends a substantial amount of time helping you improve your negotiations skills in your home life. This second addition adds eight new examples to the chapter *Knowing it, doing it, saying it*. These cover most of the common negotiation scenarios that you will meet in your home life: buying and selling your house, buying a car, buying white goods, commissioning building works and other home improvements, and renewing services such as insurance, energy provision and car breakdown cover.

Brilliant negotiations are key to a happy, prosperous life and a successful career. If somebody has something you want, if you have something that somebody else wants, or if you are in any form of dispute, then you have to negotiate with others to get a good result.

Bad negotiators pay a terrible price

If you are buying something then the title of this section is literally true! It is also true in the wider sense that your personal happiness and prosperity, and the success of your career, will be severely affected if you are a poor negotiator. Many of the most important interactions you will have with other people involve the give and take of a negotiation. Get it wrong and you will pay too much, sell too cheaply or fail to reach good compromises in disputes and in group decision-making situations. Get it wrong and you can also damage relationships with friends, loved ones, colleagues, bosses, suppliers, customers and partners ... to name but a few.

Natural negotiators are rare

There are a few lucky people who have no fear of negotiations, and relish the chance to get a great deal. This book will help good negotiators become brilliant, and show poor negotiators the path towards brilliance. If you are someone who relates to any of the following points then this is the book for you:

- I am no good at haggling.
- Being a tough negotiator isn't in my nature.
- I prefer to avoid disputes.
- I mustn't jeopardise my relationship with my opposite number.
- Using pressure to close a deal will make me no better than a door-to-door salesman.

Learn the rules of the game

Knowledge is often the best way to counteract fear. This book tells you that negotiations are best thought of as a game, and gives you the rule book. If you try to play the game without understanding these rules then you have every reason to be fearful.

> negotiations are best thought of as a game

Learn the tactics, strategies and techniques

Just like playing bridge, having understood the rules you need to learn good tactics, strategies and techniques: how to understand the context of a game within a bridge match, how to assess the strength of your hand, how to open, how to understand the cues contained in other players' bids, how to respond in your future bids, how to play your hand skilfully, and the like. Becoming a brilliant negotiator demands a wider range of tactics, strategies and techniques, but these can be learned from this book, and then honed by applying them in real negotiations.

What will you learn?

This book will equip you with everything you need to become a brilliant negotiator … except practical experience. Just some of the things you will learn are:

- How to identify the situations when you should be able to negotiate a great deal.
- How to select the right negotiating strategy and the right tactics.
- How to establish a relationship with your opponent.
- How to estimate the value of a product or service.
- How to handle deadlock.
- How to close and get commitment for a deal.
- How to apply the advice in this book to real-life situations, such as negotiating a pay rise.

Use this book in every negotiation situation

This book is not just for those involved in large set-piece business negotiations. It is equally applicable to purchasing or selling a car, settling a dispute with a neighbour, dividing up office space with a colleague, selling a product or service … in short, all the myriad negotiating situations you will face in your home and work lives.

I give real-life, pragmatic advice for real-life situations. Having read this book, you will be equipped to get what you want from a negotiation ... and a little bit more.

CHAPTER 1

The basics of
negotiations

Almost every negotiating situation is unique but this first chapter will show you how many aspects of every negotiation should be treated in the same way. These common elements are:

- Your frame of mind
- The four distinct phases within every negotiation and
- The five approaches to deal-making.

Your frame of mind

In almost all cases you should adopt the attitude that 'tough is good, tougher is better'. This is the most obvious point where

Tough is good, tougher is better

Brilliant Negotiations diverges from the advice given in almost all other negotiations books. I will not perpetuate the myths that have grown up from the win/win mindset. The truth is that no matter how tough you negotiate, as long as you behave with integrity, you will not endanger any long-term relationship you will have with the other party. There is plenty of research supporting the view that setting yourself very ambitious targets for a negotiation leads to the best results from that negotiation. You are not going to achieve those ambitious targets without being the toughest of negotiators.

> **brilliant tip**
>
> The other side must not feel like losers if you are to preserve a long-term relationship.

> if you win big and they win small then they will still feel like winners

To have a good, long-term relationship you must keep the other side's respect. This means you must not humiliate the other party and you must always behave with integrity. Remember that most people respect tough negotiators and will be proud of achieving an acceptable deal against such a negotiator. If you win big and they win small then they will still feel like winners.

The main reason that negotiators fail to be tough enough is because by nature most people wish to avoid disputes. Just remember that it is not in the nature of many parents to discipline their children when they are naughty. Similarly, it is not in the nature of many managers to discipline staff who are guilty of misconduct. To be a good parent/manager this is what you have to do. It's the same with negotiations – if you want to do the job well, you have to be tough.

The financial benefits of the right state of mind

Frequently you will be negotiating on behalf of your employer. Many companies work on a profit margin as low as 10%. In many cases every extra pound/euro/dollar you negotiate goes straight on to the bottom line. To put this in perspective, if you squeeze an extra £10K out of a negotiation that may well be the equivalent of winning a £100K contract! Even if you are negotiating for yourself then every extra pound/euro/dollar is disposable income, so you should view it as a percentage of the money left after you have paid your taxes, mortgage and the like. Hopefully this analysis will convince you that pushing all the way to get every last penny out of a negotiation is worthwhile ... and I suspect in your heart you know that the tough negotiator gets a lot more than a few pennies extra.

The four phases of negotiation

All negotiations have four distinct phases. These phases are not strictly sequential because the second and third phases tend to overlap, but all four phases tend to be present in all negotiations, from buying a washing machine, to negotiating a peace deal in the Middle East. A phase may last minutes, hours, days, weeks ... or even years, but seldom will any phase be completely missing.

> seldom will any phase be completely missing

The four phases of negotiation are *preparation, the Sharing, bargaining/haggling* and *closure and commitment*:

1 *Preparation:* You need to establish what is called the frame for the negotiation. The frame for the negotiation is the context in which the negotiation takes place. In particular, you need to discover all the issues that all your stakeholders want to achieve from the negotiation. There are many other pieces of information you need to discover, such as standard

industry practice, competitor prices, and everything you can find out about your opponent and their organisation.

2 *The Sharing*: You are face to face with your opponent. It is usually a mistake to leap straight into offers and counter offers. Your preparation, no matter how comprehensive, leaves you unsighted on many key issues. You understand your frame for the negotiation, but you do not know much about your opponent's frame. There is usually much to be gained by swapping information about your frames. It is also important in a major set-piece negotiation to start to develop a respectful relationship.

3 *Bargaining/haggling*: It is time for offers and counter offers. I suspect that many readers want to buy a negotiations book to learn these 'tricks of the trade'. I will describe a wealth of techniques that will help you get an excellent deal, which can all be used without losing the respect of your opponent.

4 *Closure and commitment*: How do you conclude the deal and how do you make it stick? There are a few key techniques to be learned which will help you close the deal without having to descend to the depths of the most despicable door-to-door salesman. I will also discuss the techniques you should use to ensure that the deal doesn't quickly collapse.

The five approaches to deal-making

It is easy to be overwhelmed by the literally infinite number of negotiating situations you can find yourself in. Surely selling a company is going to be totally different from buying a car, which is going to be totally different from resolving a dispute with an aggrieved party? Of course, every potential situation may throw up the need to be creative and flexible in order to successfully conclude a deal, but there are only five basic

there are only five basic approaches to deal-making

approaches to deal-making. The fact that there are as few as five is very helpful in managing the huge variety of different negotiating situations. The five approaches are:

1 *Auction*: If appropriate, an auction can be the best way to get the top price when selling something. This approach avoids the need to do any negotiations.

2 *The sticker price*: This is a second way to avoid the need to negotiate. This is the approach that says 'those are my terms, take them or leave them'. It is not that unusual – when you visit a supermarket you know you cannot haggle with the checkout operator over the price of your basket of goods. Parents sometimes adopt this approach with their children. In certain lines of business, for example when a company sells consultancy services, it is unusual for the customer to try to negotiate the price down. If one side has overwhelming leverage they may be well advised to adopt this simple approach ... provided they do not annoy the other side so much that they walk away.

3 *The sticker price, plus/minus a bit*: This approach is commonly used when an industry has well-established standard practices, or when you are dealing with a long-term customer, or when one side has much greater leverage. The initial offer made will contain some small room for negotiation, but both sides will know that major renegotiation of the terms is unlikely to succeed. It can sometimes be used in a situation where the sticker price may seem to be acceptable, but some leeway is allowed in order to save your opponent's face. It can be helpful to think of this approach as a lightweight application of the fourth or fifth approaches described next.

4 *Haggling*: There are two overlapping definitions of what I mean by haggling. The first is when you are not at all interested in having a long-term relationship with your

opponent, so frankly you are more interested in your opponent's money or goods than their respect. The second is when you do not rely on logic: you just want more if you are selling, or want to offer less if you are buying.

5 *Bargaining*: Compared to haggling, you want to retain your opponent's respect because you expect to maintain a future relationship. As a consequence you will be much more inclined to use arguments based on logic ... but you can (and usually should) adopt a significant amount of the haggling mindset, and if done politely you are very unlikely to lose an opponent's respect.

brilliant tip

Set yourself the most ambitious, credible targets for a negotiation.

Summary

Although every deal will provide its own unique circumstances, there are only five approaches to deal-making, of which only three involve negotiating skills. There are four clearly defined stages to the negotiating process and you will learn about these in later chapters.

The most difficult challenge the brilliant negotiator faces is to approach a negotiation in the right state of mind. In almost all situations the tougher you negotiate, the better the deal you will get. Provided you act with integrity and do not humiliate your opponent you will not lose their respect, and you will not endanger any future relationship with them.

CHAPTER 2

Preparation

Preparation is the secret weapon in negotiations. Time and again I see negotiators skimping on essential preparation work and as a direct result failing to achieve their objectives in a negotiation. This chapter takes you through your preparation process:

1 *Frame the negotiation*: Understand the context in which you are negotiating.

2 *Research*: Given that knowledge is power, you need to seek out all relevant information.

3 *Set your strategy*: Before you meet face to face there are many aspects of your strategy that can be prepared … although this must not be set in stone because you always need to retain your flexibility in negotiations.

Remember that negotiations are an investment in which you invest your time in return for some benefit. The benefit may be financial, it could be in the resolution of a conflict or it could be in reaching a decision. As with all investments, you should consciously think whether the cost and benefit of your investment are sensibly balanced. Proper preparation takes time, but will significantly increase the chances that you get a good result from the negotiation.

Framing the negotiation

What do you want out of the negotiation?

It is unlikely that a negotiator would omit to find out what financial limits they can negotiate within. It is, however, a big mistake to think that this is all a negotiator has to worry about. You are likely to find that there are many stakeholders who have needs that you will have to satisfy if your negotiated settlement is to be favourably received.

> there are many stakeholders who have needs that you will have to satisfy

Some examples where stakeholders can break a deal are:

- Is there going to be a contract that will have to be signed? I can tell you that you are a very lucky person indeed if you can find someone who will meekly append their signature to a legal document without asking you searching questions.
- If a legal agreement is going to be signed, then your contractual advisers will work under many inflexible constraints.
- Your financial department will usually have the power to veto a deal.
- In your personal life, are you willing to risk buying something your spouse hates?

You need to understand key stakeholders' views before you start negotiating, and you will often want to run a potential deal past them before closing it.

How does the negotiation relate to selling?

If you are selling, then you want to complete the sales process before you start negotiating the price and other conditions. If you are buying, you want to negotiate without having committed to purchase that particular item.

brilliant tip

When negotiating to buy a product, keep reminding the salesperson that you are still considering competitive products from other manufacturers.

If you are negotiating after one of your salespeople has convinced a customer to buy, you need to discover what concessions the salesperson has already made – and many salespeople tend to be too generous with concessions.

How does the negotiation relate to a legal agreement?

As the Hollywood film mogul Sam Goldwyn famously said, 'a verbal contract isn't worth the paper it's written on'. Sometimes a negotiation precedes the creation of a legal agreement, whilst at other times the negotiation and legal agreement are hammered out in a single process. Often there will be a clear precedent for which of these methods is appropriate for a particular negotiation. For example, in the publishing industry the negotiation is nearly always hammered out at the same time as the contract is finalised. There are advantages to doing the contract at the same time – the draft contract becomes a precise, and hopefully unambiguous, summary of what has been agreed. In addition, the deal is closed, and commitment shown, by the formal exchange of signatures.

> there are advantages to doing the contract at the same time

If the haggling, or bargaining, precedes the creation of a legal agreement then you need to be aware that negotiations can easily be reopened as you craft a legal agreement acceptable to both sides.

What will the post-negotiation relationship be?

It is very important to recognise the situations in which there will be no long-term relationship with your opponent or only a weak relationship. To be brutal, in such circumstances you don't really care if you lose your opponent's respect; although even in such circumstances most decent people will usually recoil from behaving in a way that would cause this. If you hope to have a strong long-term relationship, you must ensure you keep your opponent's respect (whilst still being an extremely tough negotiator).

brilliant tip

If you are in a position where the other party is in a dominant position, for example, you are a supplier to a long-term customer, you may want to try making them your friend because they will be less likely to exploit their dominant position if they like you. This is one of the rare cases in which you will not want to be a tough negotiator.

How will your opponent frame the negotiation?

An essential part of preparation is to put yourself in your opponent's shoes. What do you think they want out of the negotiation? How powerful do you think they will perceive their negotiating position to be?

Research

Know what the object of the deal is

This depends on the situation you find yourself in.

Selling

If you are selling something then make sure you really understand exactly what is on offer. If I had a pound for every time I have seen the seller misrepresent their offering I would be a rich man. The problem is that many offerings are constantly evolving so it is very easy to be unaware of the situation regarding

many offerings are designed to be adaptable

the latest specifications, promotions, special offers and the like. It is also easy to be out of date about what new features are going to appear at particular times in the future. To make matters worse, many offerings are designed to be adaptable, so you need to know what can be changed, at what cost, on what timescale.

Buying

If you are buying then you need to be sure that you are purchasing the most cost-effective solution to your requirement. Even something as straightforward as buying a car illustrates the complexity:

- Vehicle type – saloon, hatchback, estate, SUV, MPV ... ?
- Fuel type – diesel, petrol or hybrid?
- What engine size and power rating?
- Must-have features – air-conditioning, sat-nav, leather ... ? etc.

Disputes

What exactly are the issues in dispute? You will also need to research the history of the dispute.

Decisions

You need to find out what exactly is the nature of the decision, what are the options and what are the constraints.

For example, if you are discussing how to celebrate a special occasion with your spouse, you will need to research possible types of treat, venues and the like.

If you are discussing allocation of office space, you need to understand the needs of your people, and the needs of others. You will also need to understand all the constraints on the usage of the office space that you find is available.

Sources of information

Remember to think about all the different sources of information available to you:

● In these days of the Internet, that can be an invaluable resource.

● Find out what your network of friends and colleagues can tell you.

● Don't forget printed information – magazines, newspapers, books and the like.

Research the competition

Regardless of whether you are buying or selling, you need to understand what are the prices and features of the competition. The price you want from a buyer, or the price you are willing to pay for a product or service, is bound to be influenced by both competitive offerings and the number of potential buyers. Anyone who negotiates with a car salesman without knowing what an Internet trader is selling the car for is missing a trick.

Understand the relevant market

It may not be mandatory to follow what others in the market are doing, but in most cases it makes sense to go with the herd. For example, if you are an author you can join the Society of Authors and it will be able to tell you how your publisher's standard royalty rates compare with other publishers. An author's position is the same as many other people's – you are not going to do significantly better than the terms that are prevalent in the industry.

You should use all available sources of information. I have found the Internet to be a rich source of such intelligence. For many major markets you will find a selection of books is available. You may well find that there are people in your organisation who have relevant intelligence. You may have friends and relations who can help.

If you are involved in negotiating a dispute, then the analogous issue is to find out about any legal precedents relating to your situation.

find out about any legal precedents

Understand your opponents

Remember that knowledge is power. The sorts of information you are after include:

● The nature of the organisation you are dealing with. At the very least look at its website or ask for a brochure.

● Who will you be dealing with? Where do they stand in the organisational structure? Can you find out anything about their personality?

● Can you find out anything about the company culture and internal politics?

You will use all the sources of information that have been described in the two preceding sections. In addition, an obvious approach for large set-piece negotiations, which is surprisingly seldom used, is to ask the other side to tell you about themselves and to invite them to send you information to read. In such a situation you should offer to supply them with reciprocal information. In most circumstances you should ask who the other side are fielding in the negotiation, and ask for CVs or short biographies of their negotiators. Again, you should of course reciprocate. This approach is often a very good lead in to the sharing phase that follows.

Money matters

Before you start considering your negotiating strategy you must understand your financial position, and any other issues that underpin the point at which you need to walk away from a potential deal. It is very easy to get so carried away with the competitive aspect of bargaining that you end up closing a deal that will lose you money, or requires you to buy something you cannot afford, or resolves a dispute on terms that you should not be willing to accept.

The advice I have given may sound obvious, and some aspects may be very easy to understand, such as whether you can afford the repayments on the finance deal for a new car. Be warned, however, that understanding the full financial context can be very hard indeed. Consider the sale of a service:

understanding the full financial context can be very hard

- What are your fixed and variable costs?
- If you haven't covered your fixed costs, you will definitely need to cover your variable costs, but how small a contribution to the fixed costs are you willing to accept in this deal?
- Are the fixed costs really fixed or do they, in fact, increase with the number of sales?
- Have you remembered to cost any liabilities, especially any you are not insuring against?

brilliant tip

The point at which you decide to walk away from a deal must be properly informed by your financial situation. It is very important that you walk away from a bad deal, and your financial situation is a major issue in deciding that a deal is a bad one.

Your strategy

Having framed your negotiation and done your research, it is time to work out how you are going to approach the negotiation. There are many interlinked aspects to setting your initial negotiation strategy, so I will begin with the aspect that even experienced negotiators often get wrong.

How much leverage do you have?

Leverage refers to the balance of power between negotiators. The single most important contributor to leverage is how relaxed/desperate you are to do a deal. A desperate negotiator is in a weak negotiating position and hence has less leverage than an opponent who is more willing to walk away from the deal. You can assess how relaxed/desperate you are by working out what you will do if you fail to close a deal. Your 'walk-away' scenario, or scenarios, will be the single greatest source of leverage.

Interestingly, the importance of your walk-away scenario illustrates how stupid many organisations are in saying that an opportunity is a 'must win' ... there is no better way of crippling your negotiators.

In most situations you have more leverage than you realise ... except if you think you have a lot of leverage, in which case you have probably overestimated your position! Underestimating your leverage partly explains why so many negotiators are too timid in their aspirations for a negotiation. Overestimating your leverage explains why a negotiator who has been dealt a strong hand so often fails to secure a deal.

> you have more leverage than you realise

It is important to avoid confusing negotiating power (leverage) with personal or organisational power. Say you are an individual negotiating with a large multi-national company – you should not assume that you have less leverage than the multi-national.

Identify your deal breakers

You will want to consider your walk-away point on price. Walk-away points tend to obscure the fact that there are many issues of value other than a headline price, but they do provide a very valuable trip-wire to avoid a negotiator getting carried away and doing a deal they should have walked away from. In a negotiation, you can always take a deal that breaks your walk-away point back to your stakeholders for consideration, because your stakeholders may then decide that the totality of the deal is better than not doing the deal.

Whilst discussing the impending negotiation with your stakeholders, you need to flush out all the potential deal-breaking issues in addition to price. In large set-piece negotiations, contractual issues will be as great a threat to a deal as price.

---

brilliant example

Most organisations correctly view an unlimited indemnity in a contract as a potential threat to the survival of the organisation. As a result, indemnities are one of the most common deal-breakers.

Select your deal-making strategy

Auction

If you decide to sell by auction there will be no role for negotiations. It is most commonly used when you require a quick sale, or when you anticipate a high level of demand for what is being sold.

Sticker price

Like an auction, the sticker-price strategy leaves no room for negotiation. It is a deal-making strategy that assumes you have the leverage to dictate sales terms.

Sticker price plus or minus a bit

This deal-making strategy can be used in preference to 'sticker price' when one side is very dominant. It is often used when terms and conditions do not vary greatly within an industry (e.g. all publishers tend to use it). It is a common deal-making strategy when both sides have an established long-term relationship.

Haggling

Haggling is the best deal-making strategy when you don't care about a long-term relationship with your opponent ... being a bit crude, you don't care if they still respect you in the morning. Haggling tends to be most successful when the item being negotiated is well defined. Haggling when both price and specification are very fluid is much more difficult than the situation where the specification is known in detail.

> you don't care if they still respect you in the morning

Bargaining

Bargaining is the deal-making strategy in all other situations. It tends to be the dominant approach for large set-piece commercial, trades union and political negotiations. It has been the subject of much academic research, which is why it figures so prominently in many of the best-selling negotiations books. Many authors of negotiations books (like me) feel they are qualified to write books on the subject because of the battle scars they have gained in high-stakes bargaining. It is an important strategy, but never forget that simpler negotiations vastly outnumber large set-pieces.

Select your negotiating team and define their roles and authorities

There are a number of different roles that can be used within a negotiating team.

The lead negotiator

You must choose who will be the lead negotiator. The lead negotiator must be the only person who makes offers and counter offers. Because the lead negotiator controls the offers and counter offers, it is essential that they be able to control any other people on their negotiating team. The lead negotiator needs to explain the ground rules to others on their team and to arrange any signals that will be used covertly to communicate instructions to the rest of the team. At the very least, the lead negotiator will need a signal to tell someone to shut up.

At the very least the lead negotiator will need a signal to tell someone to shut up

There is sometimes a conflict between choosing a skilled, battle-hardened negotiator or using someone with less negotiating experience but more knowledge about the issues being negotiated. You should not under-estimate just how much extra an experienced, battle-hardened nego-tiator will be able to extract from a deal. Another advantage of using a

> they will bow out at the end of a tough negotiation

professional gun-slinger is that they will bow out at the end of a tough negotiation, leaving someone else, who has no history of having been a tough b*****d, to start building the constructive long-term relationship.

The lead negotiator's second

The lead negotiator's second is there to advise the lead nego-tiator. The second can play a number of different roles:

- They may have more domain knowledge of what exactly is being negotiated.

- In a cross-cultural negotiation the second may understand the culture (and possibly the language) of the opponent.

- The second may listen for signals from the opponent that the lead negotiator may miss in the heat of the negotiation.

- The second may play a harder or softer role than the lead negotiator as a variant of the so-called good cop/bad cop tactic.

The scribe

The scribe will record the status of what has been agreed, pos-sibly in the form of a legal agreement. It is best if there is a single scribe in a negotiation. If it is a buying/selling situation then it is traditional for the seller to provide the scribe.

A numbers person

If the financial issues underlying a deal are very complex, it can be useful to have someone with accountancy skills on your team.

Hangers on

In an important negotiation, you may find that other people try to muscle in. For example, your organisation's account manager, who looks after business with the other side, may want to be present. You should do everything you can to dissuade such people from attending. The more people present, the greater the opportunity for mistakes.

What is the ideal team?

For a large set-piece negotiation, a lead negotiator on both sides and one scribe can work very well. It is well worth asking the other side what team they intend to field, as you will not want to be vastly outnumbered. If the other side intends to come mob-handed it can be useful to suggest that both sides field more modest teams.

brilliant tip

Clarify your authority to negotiate. If you have to run a deal past anyone else in your organisation before it can be agreed, then find out beforehand and warn your opponent that this needs to happen.

Identify possible venues for the negotiation

The order of desirability for venues is:

1 home turf
2 a neutral location
3 your opponent's turf.

The importance of the venue is often overestimated, but if it worries you then insist on a neutral venue rather than accepting an invitation to your opponent's premises. If the negotiation is using the 'one negotiator each, plus a scribe' then the negotiation should usually be held at the premises of the side that is providing the scribe, or failing that at a neutral location.

If you successfully invite your opponent to your premises then resist the temptation to play silly games such as ostentatious displays of power (the big desk), or unequal positioning (my chair is higher than yours, or you are facing the sun). Remember to be very hospitable, assisting with travel arrangements, laying on decent refreshments and the like.

> resist the temptation to play silly games

Increasingly, all or part of a negotiation will be held in cyberspace, with the negotiators communicating by email. I have conducted a number of large set-piece negotiations largely in cyberspace, and have been delighted with how smoothly the process can work. Cyberspace negotiations tend to avoid misunderstandings because people usually think before they type and are much more precise in emails than they are in conversation. You will also have a complete written record to refer back to. One danger of a cyberspace negotiation is that the Sharing phase sometimes gets skimped on, but if both sides are aware of this danger it can usually be handled. I have had one negotiation where the sharing happened face to face and the bargaining was done by email, and it worked just fine. Another danger is that people can occasionally be much ruder in emails than they would be face to face; in such circumstances an immediate response of 'please don't send me flame mails' will usually work, and if they don't stop you may have to insist on meeting face to face, ignore it or consider withdrawing from the negotiation.

Prepare for haggling or bargaining

The following preparations should be made:

- You need to think if there are any reasons not to negotiate very toughly.

- You need to consider your opening position: are you going to make an opening offer or do you want to persuade the other side to open? What will you do if they refuse to make an opening offer?

- Prepare all the arguments you can use to get a better deal, and have all the evidence ready to support those arguments.

- You need to decide if you are going to limit the time you devote to the negotiation, and hence when you may need to deliver a 'take it or leave it' ultimatum.

- How will you respond to an ultimatum from your opponent?

- You need to know all your walk-away points and how willing you are to exercise a walk-away scenario.

Summary

Preparation is so important that I would strongly advise that each and every time you negotiate, you take this book down off the shelf and flip through the section headings to make sure you think about all the key issues.

The single most important part of preparation is to discover all the issues of all the stakeholders who might veto a deal.

You must find out everything you can about your opponents, both their personalities and their organisation.

You cannot negotiate effectively if you do not know what the standard practices are in the market you are involved in. Likewise, you need to know what competitors are offering, regardless of whether you are buying or selling.

Finally, you must be well prepared so that you will walk away from a bad deal. You must understand your walk-away points – how desperate you are to do the deal – and you must have a firm grip on the financials, so that you will be able to judge whether a deal is best walked away from.

CHAPTER 3

The Sharing

After preparing for the negotiation, you finally meet your opponent face to face. It is usually a mistake to rush straight into exchanging offers and counter offers. You will want to get to know your opponent, set the scene and establish some ground rules before getting stuck into the bargaining or haggling phase. For reasons that will become obvious, I refer to this as The Sharing. The Sharing phase has four objectives:

1 sharing information

2 building a relationship

3 agreeing the negotiation process

4 reducing your opponent's expectations.

Sharing information

brilliant tip

Be even handed, not competitive, when sharing information.

Both sides of the negotiation will benefit from sharing the following pieces of information:

- *How you both frame the negotiation*: It will be too early to talk about money, but sharing the non-financial issues of your stakeholders is well worth doing.

- *Discuss what is being offered and what is wanted*: Most negotiations revolve around one side offering something that the other side wants. Usually it is not a single simple thing being offered. Often the things being offered are not precisely what the other side wants; and it is not unusual for the side wanting to buy to be unclear in their own minds exactly what they want. Clarifying what might be offered, and what is wanted, is time very well spent.

- *How you are going to handle contractual issues*: You need to agree how you are going to record the agreement you reach.

- *Share industry standard terms*: Most negotiators will have researched the 'case law' of industry practice that relates to the negotiation. One of you will have optimistic cases (the seller) and the other will have pessimistic cases (the buyer), and you will both benefit from sharing them upfront.

- *Share competitor prices*: As with industry standard terms you need to share the best and worst comparative prices.

- *Are there any time pressures?* You don't want time pressures to emerge unexpectedly during the negotiation. These time pressures can cover issues such as deadlines for concluding the negotiation, validity periods for special offers, delivery times, and the like.

- *Share any relevant financial issues*: Although you haven't reached the offer and counter-offer stage, it is worth sharing key elements of your financial situations. For example, if one side in the negotiation is a cash buyer, someone is looking for particular payment terms or one party values one aspect in the financial negotiation more highly than

No surprises – negotiations can be easily derailed if a major issue
emerges that one side has known about for some time.

No surprises

another – such as an upfront payment versus royalty rate for
an author – then these are worth exposing to each other.

- *What are the potential deal breakers?* Deal-breaking issues
  must be put on the table at the earliest opportunity. This
  could be classic deal-breaking issues such as indemnities or
  it could be something unusual. The weirdest deal-breaker
  I have come across was a US company whose negotiating
  position was dominated by its fear of being sued under US
  anti-trust laws.

- *Consider sharing your walk-away scenarios*: There is no 'one-size-fits-all' advice about the desirability of telling the other side about your walk-away scenario. If they tell you about their walk-away scenario you should reciprocate, otherwise you will be implicitly acknowledging their superior leverage. But should you offer yours up first? In some situations the choice will be obvious – for example, if you are buying a car then you should mention scenarios such as 'I will be changing my car only if I get a sufficiently attractive deal'. In other situations mentioning your walk-away scenario may appear unnecessarily aggressive ... so you need to play each situation on its own merits.

  play each situation on its own merits

- *Clarify both sides' authority to negotiate*: Probably the worst surprise you can give your opponent is saying, after a deal appears to have been agreed, that someone else in your organisation has to approve the deal. Both sides should clearly describe exactly what authority they have to conclude a deal.

Building a relationship

Brilliant negotiators are always good listeners

By sharing information you have already started building a relationship. In fact, sharing information is an excellent start because many of your interactions will be non-contentious, so you have a chance to get to know each other before starting to push into more contentious areas.

You need to behave in a way that builds up trust with your opponent.

Your behaviour – what to do

Do listen carefully

Brilliant negotiators are always good listeners. Time and again I have been amazed at how even experienced negotiators either don't listen to what I am saying, or if they hear what I say, they don't remember it. An essential part of negotiations is giving and receiving cues about future negotiating positions. It is essential that you receive the cues sent by the other side.

---

brilliant example

There was a superb example of missing a cue in the US series of *The Apprentice*. The negotiation was between a team of contestants and a celebrity, where the contestants were trying to negotiate what the celebrity would offer for sale in a charity auction. The celebrity said something like:

'I would really like to get the highest amount of money of all the celebrities that are appearing on *The Apprentice*.'

I have seldom heard a clearer or more generous cue ... which the lead negotiator from that team of contestants totally ignored.

Do ask lots of good questions

There are two types of good question. The first is the equivalent of the laser-guided bomb – you ask precisely and unambiguously for a piece of information. An example might be:

Is there any advantage to you in completing the sale by a particular date?

The second type of good question is the question that invites your opponent to talk around an issue, which may gather a wealth of unexpected information. For example:

What special offers do you have at the moment that might tempt me?

With this second type of open question you should be alert to asking follow-up questions, whilst remembering to reactivate the original question if you have just dived down into a particular piece of detail.

Do use the power of silence

Politely waiting for an answer, especially if the silence drags on uncomfortably long, is a wonderful technique to draw out information. It is surprising how often the other side will blurt out something helpful to fill a silence. Be alert to your opponent using this technique on you.

> the other side will blurt out something helpful to fill a silence

Do use anecdotes to make points and build a relationship

The best negotiators I have met are very skilled at telling interesting anecdotes, which serve the dual purpose of building a relationship with their opponent, and can also indicate their approach to issues that are pertinent to the negotiation.

Do be careful talking about your personal life

If your opponent mentions details about their private life then you are not obligated to respond with details of your personal life, but they are effectively giving you carte blanche to do so. The more you know about each other then the easier it will be for both sides to anticipate how their opponent will react to particular situations. It also helps you empathise with your opponent. I don't think that sharing personal details is wrong, nor do I feel that withholding them is improper. If you are the first to mention personal details then I advise that you be sensitive to whether you are making your opponent uncomfortable – and if they are uncomfortable, then you should stop.

Do empathise with your opponent – but don't feel sorry for them

My favourite dictionary (Chambers) describes empathy as follows:

'The power of entering into another's personality and imaginatively experiencing his or her experiences'

The power of empathy is your ability to predict how your opponent will react to your proposals. The danger of empathy is that you may start to feel their pain and relate to their problems. A really good deal from your perspective should not be pain-free for your opponent. As one of my friends says, 'If I cannot see the hint of a tear in their eyes I know I haven't negotiated hard enough' ... so beware of empathy making you feel sorry for your opponent.

> beware of empathy making you feel sorry for your opponent

Your behaviour – what not to do

Don't show disrespect

Never be rude, condescending, belittling, arrogant ... I leave the reader to complete the list of behaviours that will help destroy a respectful relationship between the parties.

Don't talk too much

Good negotiators are often extroverts, so they suffer the danger of dominating the conversation. Given the importance of listening, extroverts need to remember that they may need to shut up and let the other side speak.

Don't betray confidences
It is important not to betray confidences that other parties would expect you to keep to yourself. If your opponent hears you betraying confidences, they will be quite right not to trust you completely.

Don't try to make friends with your opponent
Most people do not negotiate hard with their friends because they value their friendship more than a good deal. Consequently you do not want to be too friendly with your opponent.

There is another, subtler risk in becoming friends with your opponent. If they feel that your tough negotiations are betraying your friendship then they may get annoyed with you ... and losing your opponent's respect is a big deal.

Overcoming barriers to building a relationship
There are many situations which make it hard to develop a relationship with your opponent. You need to recognise, and overcome, such barriers.

One side is much keener to do a deal than the other
The more desperate party is going to find it hard to be relaxed. The best technique to adopt in such a situation is to treat negotiating as a game – this will help reduce your stress levels.

The two sides have some negative history
It is worth talking openly about past bad experiences and trying to gain an acceptance that both sides are committed to avoiding a repetition. This can lead to the next point ...

The two sides don't trust each other
As an example, you may be dealing with an organisation that has a reputation for aggressive business practices. As in the last

point, it is worth bringing such concerns into the open, and agreeing if any measures are suitable to build greater trust. For example, one side may warn the other that it is going to insist on some fairly draconian protection in a watertight, non-disclosure agreement, before details are given of what is being offered.

You are less experienced a negotiator than your opponent

The most successful technique is to ask for guidance from your opponent ... a difficult request for them to refuse, and a difficult position for

ask for guidance from your opponent

the more experienced negotiator to take advantage of.

One side is much more powerful than the other

For example, if an individual is negotiating with a large company, they may well feel intimidated. It is worth remembering that organisational power is not the same as negotiating power (leverage), and if one side has much less leverage they will also probably feel intimidated. This is another situation where it is best to treat negotiations as a game, in order to reduce the feelings of stress.

brilliant tip

If you behave in a confident manner, your opponent will start to believe you have a decent amount of negotiating power, and you will start to feel more confident.

If the two sides come from different cultures, and even worse if one side is a native English speaker and the other isn't

In such a situation, it is best for the lead negotiator to have a supporter who understands the other culture and language.

Agreeing the negotiation process

During The Sharing, the first thing you will want to negotiate is how you are going to conduct the negotiation.

Agree the mechanics of bargaining/haggling

Some situations may call for a single, intense, face-to-face session – the negotiating equivalent of the jury in a court case being closeted away until they reach a verdict. Other situations may be suited to weekly face-to-face meetings with telephone and email negotiations in between; whilst the other extreme involves a solely cyber-negotiation. There is no single best process: both sides must agree together what is the best process for their particular negotiation.

How will you capture what has been agreed?

This may be simple in a situation such as an aspiring author's negotiation with a publisher, where the publisher sends the author their standard contract and the author negotiates changes to that standard contract. In situations where there isn't an evolving draft contract or other form of legal agreement, the next best thing will be to keep an informal written record of key points. The increasingly common model, where much of the bargaining happens by email, facilitates this very well indeed. If you are negotiating without recourse to a written record, then both sides should agree to frequent oral summaries of the key points.

> both sides should agree to frequent oral summaries

Agree to air grievances

One of the most frequent causes of problems I have encountered is when I have unconsciously been annoying my opponent, who has bottled up their annoyance – the pressure in them then grows and grows until their frustration boils over in an emotional outburst. To avoid this happening, both sides should agree to air grievances as soon as they develop.

Discuss personal preferences and relevant past experience

Most experienced negotiators have accumulated personal preferences over the years, usually based on their experiences of what has worked well, or badly, in the past. It is worth sharing these preferences to see if you can both benefit from the past experiences you have had.

One particular area that should be discussed is the methods that both sides have successfully used in the past to overcome deadlock in the negotiation process. As an example, I have resolved many difficult issues by leaving a situation to be resolved if it occurs in the future, with an agreement to refer the issue to an independent arbitrator if both sides fail to agree.

brilliant example

Authors and publishers often find it difficult to agree a definition of what the publishing industry calls a 'competing publication'. For example, a publisher quite rightly doesn't want an author to write a similar book for a different publisher; however, the author may want to write a more general book that includes a chapter on the subject of the original book. Such a situation can be resolved by writing some general wording in the contract that the author will agree not to write a book that will significantly damage the sales of the original book, but if the two parties fail to agree on a particular issue that emerges in the future, they agree to accept the view of an independent arbitrator.

Reducing your opponent's expectations

Although it is too early to start making offers or counter-offers, The Sharing is a good opportunity to subtly reduce your opponent's expectations of how good a deal they are likely to achieve. The lower their expectations, the better the deal you can negotiate. There are many ways you can achieve this when discussing your offering, your financial situation, timescales, your walk-away scenarios, and the like.

Here are some examples of how you might achieve this:

- 'I don't have to buy now; I will be buying only if the price is attractive.'
- 'We are very busy right now, but I will try to fit your job in before the end of the summer.'
- 'You are very lucky I happen to have one in stock; they are as rare as hens' teeth.'
- 'We aren't cheap, but we pride ourselves on providing value for money.'
- 'Engineering like this doesn't come cheap.'
- 'We pride ourselves on our personal service; we don't try to compete with Internet retailers.'
- 'I will pay only a modest premium over the price I can get on the Internet.'
- 'Of course you can buy this cheaper, but if something goes wrong ...'

brilliant tip

When bluffing, stick to statements that cannot be disproved.

I am sure you have got the idea – have fun planning your own expectation deflaters!

Summary

The Sharing phase allows you and your opponent to exchange information, build a relationship and agree the negotiation process. You should also take the opportunity to say things that will reduce the other side's expectations of how much they can achieve from the negotiation.

Whilst sharing information, you should be even-handed rather than competitive. Whilst building a relationship, your prime objective should be to establish trust between yourself and your opponent. However, you should be wary about building an overtly friendly relationship as this will make it hard to be very competitive whilst haggling or bargaining. For similar reasons you should be careful not to let your empathy for your opponent translate into feeling sorry for them.

To get the most out of The Sharing, you must be a great listener, who asks lots of good questions.

CHAPTER 4

Haggling

f you do not intend to have a long-term relationship with the other side … it's time to haggle! Almost everything you purchase or sell in your private life will be susceptible to haggling. Although you cannot haggle for your basket of groceries, this is the exception rather than the rule. The great thing about haggling is that you can relax and enjoy it, because even if you make a mistake there will be no long-term damage.

> relax and enjoy it, there will be no long-term damage

You also benefit from the fact that when buying and selling, your opponent expects you to haggle – even the smartest of London jewellers will not be offended by you haggling for jewellery or designer watches.

Haggling is a game with well-established rules. The first section in this chapter provides you with a comprehensive set of these rules, which will equip you to be a very effective haggler. The last three sections explain how to answer three of the most difficult issues in negotiation:

1 How do you establish the value of something?

2 Should you make the opening offer?

3 At what level do you pitch an opening offer or your first counter-offer?

brilliant question

If you cannot bear the thought of haggling, you must at the very least ask politely 'What is your best price/offer?'

The rules of haggling

Rule 1 – Don't go into a haggling session unprepared

The single most important piece of homework is to know all the reasons why you should get a good deal – for example, if you are buying, what prices are being quoted on the Internet. One specific item of preparation you must do is encapsulated in the next rule.

Rule 2 – Set yourself a really challenging objective

There has been loads of academic research on negotiations, and time and again this research shows that the more challenging your objective, the better you will do. The more challenging your objective, the more competitive you will be in the haggling session.

Rule 3 – Be clear upfront what you want

It is much better to state clearly upfront what you want, rather than to keep slipping in new conditions as you go along. It is another example of the universal KISS principle – Keep It Simple, Stupid! This doesn't mean that you shouldn't be flexible if your opponent offers you an attractive alternative to what you originally asked for.

haggling is a battle of wills

Rule 4 – Haggling is a game

Haggling is a battle of wills, and the best way to be very competitive, but remain unemotional, is to treat it as a game.

You will often be up against someone who has been trained to haggle, or who may be part of a culture with over a thousand-year history of haggling. They will expect you to haggle, and in extreme cases they will be offended if you do not play the game.

Rule 5 – You do not have to be reasonable

Many bargaining strategies are based on rational arguments. When haggling you know that your opponent wants to get things out of the negotiation, and your objective is to minimise what they get so as to maximise what you get. It is a battle of wills where your objective is to convince your opponent that the only way to conclude a deal is to agree with one of your offers.

brilliant tip

I **want** … and if I don't get what I want then I will go elsewhere.

Rule 6 – Be rational if it suits your cause

Throw in logic whenever it supports your position. Comments such as 'I can get it cheaper on the Internet' can be deployed whenever it suits you. As the next rule states, you can even use false logic.

Rule 7 – Bluffing is absolutely fine (but try not to get caught out)

'I can buy something similar for £12,500' is almost impossible to disprove. Bluffing is an acceptable (but dangerous) strategy in bargaining. Bluffing is totally acceptable in haggling, and although you should try to avoid getting caught, you should look totally unembarrassed if you do get caught out.

Rule 8 – A bit of overacting never hurts

A bit of overacting never hurts

In this game, a bit of overacting will almost always be acceptable. I suggest you work on your look of complete astonishment – to be used when you hear your opponent's opening offer. Often the experienced haggler will overact with a touch of humour.

Rule 9 – Many questionable bargaining practices are acceptable

In the next chapter I draw boundaries as to what techniques are acceptable. For example, blatant use of your negotiating power (leverage) is seldom acceptable as a bargaining tactic, but is fine in haggling.

Borderline tactics such as 'nibbling' are also OK – nibbling is where you appear to have agreed a deal and then come back demanding additional sweeteners: 'You will throw in a full tank of petrol, won't you … surely you aren't going to lose the deal over a tank of petrol?'

Rule 10 – Use every bit of leverage you have

If you have a strong, credible walk-away scenario, then make sure your opponent is very aware of it, for example, 'If you cannot sweeten that deal then I will go back and see if your competitor can do better.'

If it is credible, then strongly encourage your opponent to think about the chances of future business from you. Likewise, if you are a regular customer then play that up for all it's worth. If you have friends to whom you may pass on a recommendation, that is worth mentioning. Phrases such as 'I work for the biggest employer in the town, so lots of people will get to know if I am happy with your service' can work well.

Rule 11 – Take your time

Realising that haggling is a game, you may be tempted to short-circuit the process. For example, you may say something silly like: 'We know we are going to end up agreeing on £15,000, let's just shake hands.' Bad tactic! £15,000 will be taken as your current offer and your opponent will work on improving from this position. You cannot hurry the process, so relax and enjoy it.

Rule 12 – Never reveal your budget

If your opponent is an experienced negotiator they will try to get you to tell them what your budget is. Keep your budget to yourself because as soon as your opponent knows what it is, you can be sure they won't let up till they have extracted the full amount from you.

Rule 13 – Don't be fooled into meeting them halfway

If your opponent offers to meet you halfway, then take halfway as their current offer and continue haggling from there.

Rule 14 – Make smaller and smaller concessions

Psychologically you want to indicate that you are reaching the end of your flexibility by making your concessions decrease towards zero. For example, in the motor trade a salesman may indicate the end of his concessions by saying something like: 'Well I could throw in mats and mudflaps.'

The next rule is the flipside of this technique.

Rule 15 – Consider breaking through the other side's preferred 'best offer'

Your opponent will often apply Rule 14 to you so you will get a clear idea of what appears to be their best offer. You may decide that it is acceptable, or you can try to break through this offer to see if there is a better offer to be had. There is nothing to be lost (but your time) by trying to break through what they are signalling is their best offer. The following are some possible techniques:

- 'That is more than I am willing to pay. The highest I will offer is £13,500, and I will shake your hand on that figure now.'

- 'We are clearly not going to be able to do a deal. I will see if I can get a better deal elsewhere' or 'I need to talk to my wife/husband because this is much more than we wanted to pay' ... you then leave them to stew for a period of time and come back at a later date to see if they are willing to move.

- 'I am a cash buyer who can do a deal right now, you are going to have to do better than that' ... or maybe 'a lot better than that'.

- 'Can I talk to your boss?' ... often if you can change the person you are haggling with, your new opponent will be willing to make concessions to show that they have the authority and skill to do a deal.

If you think they are really not going to move much then maybe, 'That's quite an attractive offer, and if you will throw in an extended warranty (or something else you want) then I will do the deal.' Or maybe, 'If you are willing to pay the postage then I will accept your price.' As you can always decide in the end to accept their original offer there is usually nothing to be lost by having a go.

> there is usually nothing to be lost by having a go

Rule 16 – Silence is a great tactic

People find silence very uncomfortable and there is no better way that you can politely apply this amount of pressure. Just sit there silently appearing to mull over what the other side has offered and frequently your opponent will sweeten the deal for you.

Rule 17 – If you can get an auction going then do so

If you are buying and you have more than one potential supplier, or if you are selling and have more than one person interested in buying, then you should play one off against the other(s). There is nothing like an auction for getting the best deal … competing buyers and sellers often get carried away in the desire to win the deal.

Rule 18 – Timing is crucial

If you are buying a car it is worth finding out when the garage's accounting period ends. Often dealers rely on substantial bonuses from the car manufacturers that are tied to specific targets. If the dealer is short of their target, they may be willing to sell you a car below its cost price to make their quota. Many organisations face similar pressures … there are few companies that aren't keen to make a deal just before their financial year ends.

There are other obvious timing issues to bear in mind, for example you want to buy garden furniture at the end rather than the beginning of summer ... and the same applies to motor bikes and many other items; but, of course, you want to buy cavity wall insulation in the height of summer. If your purchase or sale is seasonal, then sell in the high season and buy in the low season.

Likewise, you may choose a particularly quiet day or time of day to haggle, as your opponent is more likely to push that extra yard for a deal if business is slack. Alternatively, if you are at an antiques or flea market, then stall-holders are often more receptive to haggling at the end of the day.

Rule 19 – If things go wrong after you close the deal you can renegotiate

you are entitled to start haggling again for compensation

It is not at all uncommon after you have concluded a deal that things do not go as promised: delivery is late; it's the wrong colour; it's scratched; it has faults; it breaks down; etc. If things go wrong you are entitled to start haggling again for compensation. Most companies do not want unsatisfied customers so will have a budget for remedial action to make you happier – but that money is earmarked for those who moan ... loudly!

A common mistake a lot of negotiators make in such circumstances is to fail to state precisely what they want their opponent to do for them. Making a clear, reasonable demand is much more likely to get you a good result. Something like 'it is the wrong colour, either replace it with the specification I ordered or pay me £500 to keep the wrong colour' is the right approach.

Rule 20 – Don't get emotionally attached to the object of the haggling

When buying you are much better placed if you are willing to walk away from the deal. Try not to get emotionally attached to what you are buying.

Rule 21 – Never get angry

If a negotiation turns into an argument you are very unlikely to get what you want. The only time anger can work is when you are complaining about the delivered item when you are trying to get some compensation. If possible you should simulate the anger so you remain rational enough to have a clear objective about the level of compensation you are after.

Rule 22 – Never be unreasonable

There is a narrow dividing line between an ambitious offer in a haggle and an unreasonable demand. Unless you are in a market bazaar you should stick to the credible side of the line.

Rule 23 – Be ready to 'flash the cash'

Although I leave the general discussion of closing deals to a later chapter, I will single out one great technique. An excellent way

Be ready to flash the cash

to close a deal is to pull out a wad of banknotes for the price you want to pay and thrust them into your opponent's hand. You may be surprised how effective this can be in an appropriate situation, such as when you are buying something from a private seller.

> the most difficult issues are all to do with money

The rules of haggling have explained how you can play the game to achieve a great deal. But how do you know what is a great deal? The most difficult issues facing a haggler are all to do with money. How do you know what is a reasonable price to have as your target to close the deal at? Should you make the opening offer, or should you invite your opponent to make the first move? If you decide to make the opening offer, what price should you open at? If the other side opens, what should your first counter-offer be? The remaining sections in this chapter answer these tricky questions.

How to value something

This section is as applicable to bargaining as it is to haggling. It is also applicable to the situation where you are going to set a price and stick to it (sticker price), or when you are going to set a price and then allow only a small amount of negotiation (sticker price plus or minus a bit).

What is a fair price?
If there is a clear market price then find out what it is
Time and again I stress the importance of research. By using the Internet, looking at printed advertisements, talking to sales brokers (such as estate agents), you should get a good idea what the market prices for many items are. If you do better than that market price you are doing well.

What do you do if there isn't a clearly identifiable market price?

Valuing a unique item

Although you may not be able to find a clear market value for an item, you may be able to find other ways to determine a value. Say you are selling a company, there are a number of guidelines that are widely applied to valuing a company. One can buy books, software models, and the like, to assist you in a valuation. Many of these tools will value a company on key issues such as market capitalisation, or the projected earnings power over some period (say ten years) plus a valuation of assets. Assets can be tangible items such as buildings and stocks, or intangible but saleable items such as brand names, customer lists, goodwill and the like. Other unique items may also have widely published mechanisms to help you value them: for example, during the (lunatic) dotcom boom web-based businesses were often valued according to the number of hits they got per day.

There are a number of other techniques for helping to value a unique item:

- *By analogy*: Often you will be able to say this item is worth more/less/the same as this other item which sold for a known amount. Talking to an experienced estate agent, I found that he heavily used this technique.

- *Consult an expert*: Often the expert uses a mixture of analogy and intuition to make their estimate.

- *Sell by auction*: One solution that can be appropriate is to cut out the haggling and use an online auction site such as eBay or a physical auction house to sell the item.

- *What would I pay?* Obviously you can do this only if you are not too emotionally attached to an item, but asking yourself (and your friends and colleagues) what they would pay can be very instructive.

The following points describe how aggressive you can be in the price you wish to close the deal at.

Is it a buyers' or sellers' market?

A classic example of this phenomenon would be a booming property market. If prices are rising rapidly then few houses will be sold for significantly less than their asking price. In comparison, in a flat or falling market, properties will be susceptible to aggressive haggling.

How are supply and demand balanced?

If supply exceeds demand then the balance of power lies with the buyer, and if demand exceeds supply then the seller holds the whip hand.

Did the buyer make an unsolicited approach to the seller?

Using the example of the sale of a company – if a buyer asks the seller to sell, rather than the seller putting the company on the market, then the seller is in a much stronger position to get a high price.

Who is under the tightest time pressures?

The stronger the time pressure someone is under, the less aggressive they can be in obtaining the best price. For example, if you are selling bulky items that are cluttering up your house, you may decide that it is worth asking competitive prices just to clear them out of the way.

How good is your walk-away scenario?

If you have a strong walk-away scenario then you will definitely have good leverage and you should be aiming to haggle aggressively.

Know when to be ambitious

The buying/selling world breaks down into six cases:

1 If you are selling something that is far from unique then you will be lucky to get a price better than the market value.

2 If you are buying something that isn't rare then if you can bide your time and buy when some of the conditions outlined above are in your favour, you may get a very good price.

3 If you are selling something rare and desirable you should get a good price.

4 If you are selling something rare that a few people might want, but you are willing to wait, you should aim for a good price.

5 If you are buying something rare and desirable then be prepared to pay a premium (or be prepared to live without it).

6 If you are after something rare of limited desirability then the good haggler may do well ... keep your nerve and try not to show how badly you want it.

To open, or not to open?

The advantage of letting your opponent open

Given that most negotiators are not aggressive enough, the chances are that your opponent will open too low when selling, or too high when buying. If you then respond with an aggressive counter-offer, the bargaining phase is off to a good start.

The advantage of opening

Confident negotiators often open because if you aggressively open you can start the bargaining phase in a dominant position. If your opponent seems a confident personality, then this stratagem is unlikely to work.

There is no 'one-size-fits-all' advice. The comforting thing is that both opening, and not opening, have advantages, so you can maximise the possibilities in either case.

> there is no 'one-size-fits-all' advice

If the value of the item under negotiation is unclear, try to get your opponent to open

In addition to the likelihood that your opponent will open timidly, there is a good chance they will mistakenly value the item too low (when selling), or too high (when buying). If your opponent seems inexperienced then this is a particularly attractive approach. You will want to prompt them to open by comments such as 'What's your best offer?', or perhaps better 'What do you think it's worth?', or 'What would you accept?', or 'What's your budget?', or 'You must have some idea how much you want/are willing to pay?'

Opening offers and counter-offers

This section offers you clear advice on how to pitch your first offer.

The classic opening gambit

> it doesn't matter if your offer edges into incredible territory

The classic advice is to make your first offer or counter-offer as the highest (if you are selling) or lowest (if you are buying) figure that is credible. To be brutally honest, it doesn't matter if your offer edges into incredible territory … that is a much less damaging mistake than pitching your opening offer too cautiously. There are, however, situations in which the classic advice is the wrong advice and I'll now explain these situations.

When you want an auction to set the final price

If you are selling on an online auction site or if you hope to be able to play one buyer off against another, then you can open at a knock-down price. This usually attracts multiple bidders and sets the best environment for a bidding frenzy.

When you want a (reasonably) quick sale

There are two obvious approaches to selling something like your house. You can price it just below the market price, which almost guarantees a quick sale and you can be quite aggressive in resisting pressure to further reduce the price once you have one or more buyers interested – indeed you may get multiple buyers bidding above the offer price. Alternatively, you can set an optimistic price 'because I can always reduce the price later'. The second method may lead to someone who really wants the house paying your price, but usually leads to you reducing the price at a later date, by which time your house has missed the buzz of being new to the market.

In a market bazaar

Opening offers in this situation tend to be:

- unbelievable, and ...
- determined by local custom (often hundreds or even thousands of years old).

So ask someone familiar with local customs for advice ... and brush up on your overacting.

I am now going to say something that may seem totally out of character. If you are a tourist in an under-developed country then you have to haggle because to refuse to do so will confuse the trader (at best) or be considered rude (at worst). However, please remember that the money involved means much more to the trader than it does to you, so don't compete for the lowest possible price – give them an extra bit of profit.

Summary

The essence of haggling is **I want**. If you have logical arguments to use to get what you want, that is fine, but if you don't, you need to pit your will and skill as a negotiator against your opponent so that you get a better deal than they do. If you treat this battle of will and skill as a game, you will be able to be very competitive without getting emotional.

When valuing an item you can either research the prices of similar items, or if the item is unique you can search for an analogy to compare it with, consult an expert, sell by auction or work out what you would be willing to pay.

When buying or selling an item, the most important thing to know is when you can be ambitious on price. The buying/selling world breaks down into six cases which show how the laws of supply and demand will determine when you should be ambitious in your haggling.

If the value of an item is unclear it is best to encourage your opponent to make the opening offer. In other situations it is less clear if it is best to make the opening offer. If your opponent opens they may well be too timid, which will be to your benefit. If you open then you can confidently set the agenda on price. This means you can benefit regardless of whether you make the opening offer or not.

CHAPTER 5

Bargaining

I f you want a long-term relationship with the other side, it is time to bargain! If you are involved in a dispute in your private life, or you are buying from or selling to friends, relations or a long-term supplier, then you will want to bargain rather than haggle. Bargaining is also the preserve of all major set-piece negotiations for large commercial deals, trades union disputes, diplomatic negotiations, and the like.

You must understand the principles of bargaining, because these will give you numerous pointers that will help make you a skilled negotiator. You also need to be armed with knowledge of all the cunning tactics that you can deploy against your opponent. You must also learn how to handle that thorniest of issues – deadlock.

The principles of bargaining

Never give something for nothing

The structure of an offer goes along the lines of:

IF I give you X THEN will you give me Y?

For example:

IF I give you a three-year deal THEN will you give me a 10 per cent discount?

As a good negotiator you must ensure that you value what you are getting at least as much as you value what you are offering.

A slightly more advanced version of this is to make your demand very precise, but your offer a bit fuzzy. For example:

IF you knock a thousand pounds off the price THEN I could accept a lower specification.

Obviously you will benefit if your offer is something your opponent values but doesn't cost you much ... for example offering a three-year deal costs you nothing if you wanted a three-year deal in the first place.

Win/win is a great principle – for individual offers

In the negotiation as a whole you should hope to come away with a bigger slice of the cake than your opponent; however, in individual offers and counter-offers win/win can be used to make the cake bigger. Finding things to offer that cost you little, and asking for things that cost your opponent little, will allow you to benefit from the fact that you have avoided the negotiation being a zero-sum game. A zero-sum game is where the other side has to lose in order for you to win, because the size of the cake is fixed.

> you have avoided the negotiation being a zero-sum game

Some illustrations of items that can be used in win/win offers:

- *Customer references*: If a supplier is in the 'early adopter' phase of their product lifecycle they will usually be anxious to quote credible customer references. Being a reference customer costs a buyer very little effort, and the threat of not being able to say good things about a product or service can be a powerful lever if anything goes wrong in the future.

- *Payment terms*: There are a vast number of permutations by which payment terms can be arranged to help a cash-strapped company with its cashflow. Cash, rather than credit terms, or payment schedules are amenable to being bargained with.

- *Demonstrating that you are a good payer.* Many sellers of products and services are dogged by late payers. You can show you will be a good payer by offering penalties in the event of late payment.

- *Timescales*: For one side, time may be money, while the other side may be happy to be flexible.

- *Guarantees*: If you are confident in your offering then something akin to a money-back guarantee can be an important offer that is unlikely to cost you anything. Likewise a 'try before you buy' offer can be a cheap and effective way to help a deal along.

- *Large orders and multi-year deals*: Can be much more valuable to one side than they cost the other.

brilliant tip

Ask for concessions in situations when the cake is big. It is easier for your opponent to agree a concession that applies only when times are good. As an example, authors tend to be paid on a sliding scale of royalties that increases as sales grow. Many publishers will agree to an additional top rate if a book gets into best-seller quantities.

Maintain momentum

I have seen a lot of bargaining sessions that seem to progress more and more slowly as time passes. It is very important to maintain a sense of urgency. Agreeing a plan of the negotiating schedule; agreeing deadlines by which issues will be agreed; demonstrating a willingness to rearrange other meetings so that

> it is very important to maintain a sense of urgency

future negotiating sessions can happen quickly; the use of email and telephone between face-to-face meetings; one or both parties staying overnight so that the bargaining session can carry on late into the evening; are some examples of the techniques you will need to use to maintain momentum.

Ensure that everything that has been agreed is recorded

If possible, try not to rely on you and your opponent having the same memory of what has been agreed in the past. If a legal agreement is being drafted as you go along then this should not be a problem. Failing that, be sure to take written notes and get your opponent's agreement to them as you go along. Not only will this save a lot of time, but it can avoid either side getting emotional and accusing their opponent of breaking their word.

This principle is so important that I have frequently used a member of my team (the scribe) whose sole job is to record the state of the agreement. For large set-piece negotiations I would always recommend having such a scribe – a person who ideally has contract-drafting experience.

Perceptions are the only reality

Negotiators involved in the bargaining phase are usually under a lot of pressure. It is very easy for your opponent to misinterpret what you are saying or what your attitude is. I have seen people take offence over things I have said that I really had not expected. Never blame your opponent for getting the wrong end of the stick: calmly try to correct the perception you have created.

Offer your opponent alternatives

This is a key principle for the brilliant negotiator. For example:

Is the lowest price possible more important to you than a good warranty?

will often elicit a cue from your opponent that helps you frame an offer.

Plan your cues, and listen hard for cues from your opponent

Cues are hints about your attitude to future offers or your future actions. You should treat the cues you offer with the same degree of thought you would give to a specific offer.

Always be alert to listen to the cues your opponent sends you. Cues will often be sent to you unconsciously by your opponent, so they won't come with a clearly identifiable 'and here is a cue' as an introduction. Having heard a cue you must analyse what it means for you. Here are some examples of cues and how they might be interpreted.

Cue: *'I had a lot of problems with my previous service provider.'*

Analysis: Your opponent is probably looking for quality of service as a higher priority than price. Anything that you can offer that reduces the risks to the customer of poor service (e.g. penalty clauses) will be highly valued by the customer. Remember to stress the strength of your outstanding track record, and offer customer references.

Cue: *'Price isn't necessarily my biggest issue.'*

Analysis: Excellent! Immediately start probing for what are their major issues and make offers that will be attractive to them.

Cue: *'I am very busy at the moment.'*

Analysis: Anything that makes the buying or selling process painless will be very well received. Don't waste their time with protracted discussions or social chatter. Don't give them huge amounts of paperwork to read. Don't expect them to call you – you will probably have to do most of the chasing.

Cue: *'What is your lead time for delivery?'*

Analysis: They have some time pressures, so probe for how extreme they are. Do their time pressures put you at an advantage or disadvantage? Proceed accordingly.

your opponent is probably risk averse

Cue: *'How long have you been in business?'*

Analysis: Your opponent cares about long-term support. If you can offer a guarantee underwritten by an independent insurance company this will be well received. Your opponent is probably risk averse, so any offer that reduces risk will probably be well received.

Cue: *'Do you have many more issues?'*

Analysis: Your opponent is getting annoyed with how long the bargaining process is taking.

Know when to walk away from a bad deal

There are three techniques at your disposal:

1   Never forget your walk-away points.

2   Always compare the deal on offer with your walk-away scenario.

3   Never lose sight of the potential financial downside of a deal.

You will usually be negotiating within the context of walk-away points that were decided in advance. Although walk-away points do not take account of the ways your views may change as a negotiation progresses, they provide an essential safeguard against doing a bad deal. If you are offered a deal that breaks your walk-away points, but which you feel is better than no deal at all, you should take it back for consideration by your stakeholders.

If you don't have walk-away points there is a very real danger that you may get carried away by the excitement and competitiveness of a negotiation, and end up doing a deal that you would have been better to walk away from. The second and third items listed above will help ensure that you avoid this pitfall.

The fact that you should compare any deal on offer with your walk-away scenario is not surprising – if doing the deal is worse than the alternative, then you should walk away from the deal.

The point of not losing sight of your potential financial downside is much subtler and more difficult to apply. The precise value of a deal to the buyer or seller is often very difficult to work out. A few of the subtleties are:

● Are there risk elements (e.g. in offering a fixed price for a building contract), and how do you quantify those risks in money terms?

● What are the implications for cashflow, and how do you quantify them?

● If you are negotiating a multi-year deal, how much do you discount future years?

● If you are doing the deal partly in the hope of further work, how do you value that possibility of future profit?

● Many non-financial items like timescales have a knock-on financial impact. How do you quantify those additional costs?

● If you have to offer warranties, indemnities, penalty clauses, and the like, are you going to insure against them, or if you take the risk how do you quantify the value of that risk? This can be particularly hard because issues such as indemnities can be of low risk but potentially very high cost.

● If you are gaining non-financial benefits, such as an agreement to act as a customer reference, how highly do you value them?

A former employer of mine regarded these financial issues as such a minefield they used to mandate that all major negotiations included an accountant in our bargaining teams. If you don't have the luxury of skilled financial support then there will be times in a bargaining session when you need to take time out in the negotiation to discuss financial issues with an expert from your organisation.

brilliant tip

Bad deals are so damaging that in a borderline case you should walk away.

Use rational arguments that support your cause

As an example, if you are selling your company you might quote a figure of asset value plus a factor of 15 times annual profits. You then can argue that the buyer is likely to expand profits considerably because they can reduce costs by rationalising the cost bases between your company and the buying company, or by bringing in new investment to strengthen the product portfolio. You are then into a discussion of how much you should inflate current profits in the calculation.

you should have researched figures that flatter your position

Likewise if you want to create analogies or comparison with other competitors, you should have researched figures from companies that flatter your position.

Be flexible

One of the dangers of doing proper preparation is that you will naturally be more comfortable if the bargaining phase stays within the confines of the scenarios you have already thought about. If you think of your prepared scenarios as a box, you must be willing to think outside that box.

Bargaining tactics

Bargaining tactics can be thought of as the 'tricks of the trade' for the negotiator.

brilliant tip

Just because you have started bargaining, don't think that The Sharing is over. Keep listening, asking lots of open questions, and saying things that reduce your opponent's expectations.

Reciprocity

If your opponent makes a demand then it is worth considering if there is an analogous situation that applies from your point of view that can lead to a counter-offer along the lines of:

IF I agree to that THEN it would be reasonable for you to give me an equivalent concession.

Reciprocity can be used very effectively in the tricky area of indemnities. If your opponent asks to have a risk to themselves removed by you giving them an indemnity, then it is entirely reasonable for you to request an indemnity to address a risk that you face. Likewise if your opponent says that an unlimited indemnity is effectively 'betting the company' and hence they want to cap the indemnity, then you should ask for reciprocal caps on any indemnities that you are having to offer.

Silence

Although I have mentioned silence as a rule of haggling, it is such a terrific tactic that I felt it merited repeating. Just waiting quietly as if pondering a point, or awaiting an answer to a question, will often make your opponent so uncomfortable that they will inadvertently blurt out some valuable information or, in the best case, a revised offer.

Obviously you need to train yourself to comfortably sit out your opponent's silences.

Praise behaviour that benefits you

You can apply similar techniques that you use to train a dog to reinforce behavioural traits that benefit you. For example, you might praise a concession as being 'a creative approach'; your opponent giving you useful intelligence might be something that you 'find fascinating'.

The strategic apology

You are unlikely to get through a major set-piece bargaining session without making some major mistakes. The strategic apology is a very important tactic for repairing the damage a mistake can inflict on the relationship with your opponent. An unreserved apology will seldom be accepted ungracefully. I must stress the word unreserved … there must be no excuses, no ifs, ands or buts, to try to save face. You don't need to grovel, but you need to get as close to grovelling as you can without appearing to overact. If the apology is totally sincere then all the better, but accepting the full blame when, in fact, the situation is 'six of one and half a dozen of the other' can be equally effective.

> you need to get as close to grovelling as you can

If things are going badly, for example you have a row with your
opponent, you can stress to your opponent that you should both
look to the future, rather than dwelling on the mistakes of the past.

Good cop/bad cop

A classic ploy involves two negotiators, one playing it very hard
(who issues the threats) and another playing the conciliator (who
makes the offers). When I trained as a negotiator I was told that
this was an unacceptable technique. My objections to this tactic
are entirely pragmatic:

● It requires two negotiators, which is often too expensive to

Good cop/bad cop

justify, and provides plenty of opportunity for them to get confused as to who is in charge.

- It involves play-acting, and this can easily cause the cops to make mistakes.

- It is trivially easy to spot, and the cops will look like idiots when their opponent tells them to stop doing the 'good cop/ bad cop' routine. You are then left with one negotiator too many.

There is, however, a variant of this tactic which works very well indeed.

The third-party mandate

Again, my trainer told me not to use this tactic, a view I have come to reject. In this tactic the bad cop isn't present at the negotiation, but their views are reported to show how reasonable and conciliatory the negotiator is being. The third party can be the boss, the chairman, our lawyers, my wife/husband, life partner, business partners ... the list is almost endless, and you don't even have to limit yourself to using just one. This tactic can manifest in many ways, just a few examples of which are:

- 'Our lawyers would never let us agree to sign an unlimited indemnity.'

- 'My wife has told me I cannot spend more than £10,000.'

- 'My boss is totally irrational when it comes to vendors who won't offer ... .'

- 'My boss will kill me if I agree to ... .'

- 'That is outside my authority to agree, I will have to put it to our Board, and they will probably then reopen other issues we have agreed.'

The quotes from the third party can be true, or you can bluff ...

Bluffing

I cannot think of another part of business life where a person with integrity would consider lying ... sorry, bluffing. It is acceptable to treat bargaining as a game – your opponent will not think the worse of you for treating it as a game – and bluffing is an accepted tactic in the game.

> bluffing is an accepted tactic in the game

The rules of bluffing are as follows:

- Your opponent should not be able to disprove a bluff.
- Bluffs should be credible.
- Do not bluff too much.
- If you get caught, then carry it off with chutzpah.

Ultimata, threats and walk-outs

I tend to think of these tactics as the dark side of bargaining. There are a number of important issues you must understand.

First, ultimata and threats cover a spectrum of possibilities. If I mention the word ultimatum to you, the first thing that springs to mind is someone saying: 'That is my final offer, take it or leave it.' This example is the nuclear end of the ultimatum spectrum, which would obviously be used only in extremis. A less extreme example would be to say: 'I must insist that you get me that information before we meet tomorrow.' Exactly the same spectrum applies to threats. In addition, threats can be explicit – 'This issue is a deal-breaker for me' – or they can be implicit – 'I am not comfortable parking this issue because it is very important to me.'

Second, these tactics are dependent on the stage you have reached in the negotiation. They tend to be much more accept-able if you have reached deadlock, or are trying to close a deal. I will return to this point in the sections on deadlock and closing. Using any of these tactics early in a bargaining session is very risky.

Third, they depend on the nature of the negotiation you are involved in. I have been involved in many commercial bargaining sessions and I have never witnessed a walk-out. However, I spent ten years as a trades union negotiator, and witnessed more than a few walk-outs. Just looking at the news, one sees frequent walk-outs in diplomatic negotiations. One reason for walk-outs being common in trades union and diplomatic negotiations is that one or both sides may have to show how tough they are being to their stakeholders. It is no use a trades union doing a deal with management if that deal is then rejected in a vote by its membership. Walk-outs tend to be more common in situations where the bargaining process is somewhat stylised ... for example, trades union negotiations have very specific customs and style, and a walk-out is an accepted part of those customs.

Last, many people seem to think that these tactics have to be used in a heightened emotional state, usually showing visible anger. They are much more effective if delivered with the utmost calm and politeness, or in a style of 'more in sorrow than in anger'.

brilliant tip

A show of anger can be helpful. If you come across generally as very controlled and polite then a visible display of passion or anger will have a very strong impact on your opponent, and may well lead to the desirable position where your opponent tries to placate you. This tactic works best if used very occasionally; only when your anger is clearly justified; and you do not lose control of yourself and say something that you regret.

Read your opponent's mood

Negotiators who are naturally attuned to other people's moods, and who are good at reading body language, tend to be at a considerable advantage. If your opponent is in an excited or optimistic state they will be in a receptive mood to proposals. At the very least you need to notice when the other side's attention is wandering, in which case you will want to consider using the next tactic.

Time out

There are a number of situations when you will benefit from calling for a time out, where both sides go off into separate rooms. Some examples of situations that will benefit from this approach include:

● To give yourself or the other side a rest.

● To discuss an issue amongst your negotiating team in private.

● To contact your bosses, lawyers or financial experts to seek guidance or approval.

● To do some research to find out relevant information.

● To admonish one of your negotiating team, for example if your scribe suddenly fancies themselves as a negotiator.

● To disrupt the flow of your opponents. If they are getting the upper hand, then a time out may well be a chance for you to regroup and for them to lose their concentration ... a bit like a tennis player disputing a line call!

> ### ⚙ **brilliant** tip
>
> Make use of informal sessions. I have seen many breakthroughs in deals occur whilst both parties are standing outside a building having a cigarette break, or over lunch or having a drink in the evening. You must never drop your guard completely in such settings, but you may well listen to, and suggest, possibilities that you or your opponent would not suggest in a formal session.

Up-sell and cross-sell

Remember that the bargaining phase can be a great opportunity to up-sell or cross-sell to your opponent:

- 'For a modest additional payment we can include a .... .'
- 'If you are willing to sign up for three years' support straight away we could .... .'
- 'We also sell a service that would allow you to .... .'
- 'Why don't I arrange for you to talk to one of our experts on that subject.'
- 'Have you considered getting the upholstery treated to prevent staining?'
- 'Because our product is so reliable we are able to offer an extended warranty at very competitive rates.'

Seek competitive intelligence

Your organisation will be very interested in intelligence about areas where the opposite side might be receptive to buying its other products and services. Also the opposite side is likely to have been talking to your competitors and may inadvertently be indiscreet enough to give you valuable intelligence about your competitors' offerings, product pricing, weaknesses, strengths, and the like.

Reduce risk to the other side

It is all too easy to concentrate in a bargaining session on concrete issues such as price, delivery times, and the like. This approach ignores one of the main reasons your opponent will not agree to your deal, which is fear. Fear takes many forms:

- Fear of wasting money
- Fear that you will regret the deal
- Fear that your organisation will regret the deal
- Fear that an item being purchased will not work properly
- Fear that promises made when making a deal will not be kept.

A very good tactic is to make offers that reduce your opponent's fear:

- No-quibble money-back offer if not satisfied
- Break-points in contracts
- Guarantees
- Offer of replacement rather than repair
- Staged payments (e.g. 'buy now, pay later' for the buyer or an upfront payment for the seller)
- Try before you buy
- Warranties
- Indemnities
- Penalty clauses.

Counter tactics

There are two reasons for understanding all the available negotiating tactics. Obviously you can choose to use them on your opponent. Of equal importance is that you can spot your opponent using them on you. Knowing how your opponent wants you to react allows you to counter the tactic ... boy, can that be fun!

you can just not make the hoped-for response

There are a number of ways you can counter tactics. You can just not make the hoped-for response. For example, you will sit comfortably through a silence, rather than blurting out something useful to your opponent; or you can resist the temptation to appease your opponent's anger. In other situations, such as when your opponent tries to reduce your fear, you can be grateful for their professionalism. In a few situations you may wish to expose the tactic: for example, you should expose the use of 'good cop/bad cop'.

Handling deadlock

Many of us shy away from conflict; as a result, deadlock is the area that scares many inexperienced negotiators the most. The first thing you can do is spot that deadlock is approaching and head it off.

Throw out lots of options

Now is a critical time to be creative and 'think out of the box'. As an example from my own experience, I once avoided a deadlock situation by saying: 'Have you thought about leasing rather than outright purchase?'

What if you aren't feeling creative? In such a situation you can use the following approach.

Ask lots of (open) questions

This buys you time, and gets you potentially useful intelligence. It also keeps your opponent talking, which will help defuse any frustration they are feeling.

Assume the worst has happened and you have a deadlock, with neither side willing to move. What can you do?

Agree a rational process to resolve the deadlock

A rational process is often as powerful as a rational argument. Some rational processes are:

- Bring in an arbitrator. Arbitration can be advisory or binding. It can also be unconstrained or 'pendulum'. In pendulum arbitration, an arbitrator has to choose to agree fully with one side or the other's position.
- You divide, I choose.
- Let's take turns.
- Toss a coin.
- Split the difference.

Issue an ultimatum

This is usually best expressed in the form 'this is my best and final offer (BAFO), take it or leave it'. In most situations it is best to resist the temptation to walk out after delivering an ultimatum.

An ultimatum is obviously a high-risk strategy that works best if your opponent wants the deal more than you do. What do you do if you want the deal more than they do?

Invite your opponent to give you their BAFO

Not a common tactic, but almost always better than the alternative which is ...

Capitulate

If you would rather do the deal on their terms than walk away, then it is better to capitulate than let false pride drive you into walking away from the deal.

Of course if you prefer your walk-away scenario, you are free to ...

Walk away

They may run after you with a better offer, or come back at a later date. A less drastic version of this technique is to …

Agree to sleep on it

A surprisingly effective tactic is to part amicably and see if you or your opponent can think of a way out of the impasse. Not surprisingly, this is a particularly effective tactic when one or both sides are very tired.

> a surprisingly effective tactic is to part amicably

Brilliant do's and don'ts

I complete this chapter with a list of brilliant do's and don'ts. Many of these are fairly obvious, but a few are quite subtle.

Do correct mistaken perceptions immediately

Some opponents may accidentally, or deliberately, misinterpret what you say. You must correct them straight away. Be on the look out for them repeating the same misinterpretation, and correct them each and every time.

brilliant example

I was once negotiating to write a number of documents for a customer. To reduce the customer's risk, I offered to write one document at my own risk. After the document was written, and after we had agreed a price per document, the customer misinterpreted my offer as an offer to write the first document for free. I had to correct this misinterpretation a number of times.

Do use a contract to agree divorce terms upfront

While you are on speaking terms with your opponent you should use the opportunity to agree what will happen if things go so badly wrong that you may no longer be on speaking terms. A good contract lawyer should guide you on such conditions. If you don't have the support of a good contract lawyer then you will need to proactively write what is, in effect, a pre-nuptial agreement.

Don't get emotional

Unless you consciously decide that an emotional outburst is called for, you will do much better emulating Mr Spock from *Star Trek*. The best bargainers rely on logical rather than emotional arguments.

Don't become too emotionally committed to doing a deal

I am sure we have all seen bidders getting carried away in an auction. Just as bidders can get caught up in 'auction fever', negotiators can be infected with 'deal fever'. This is why you must always keep comparing the deal on offer with your walkaway scenario. Don't be one of the many negotiators who do the deal that they, or their organisation, live to regret.

Don't lose control of your temper

This is the extreme end of the emotional scale, but is worth singling out because I have seen more than a few negotiators damage their position significantly by losing their tempers. When someone loses control they may say anything ... and frequently do!

Don't retaliate

If your opponent loses their temper, or does something that makes you angry, then it is usually best to resist the temptation to retaliate. Remember that you are Mr Spock.

cock-ups are far more common than conspiracies

One point that is well worth remembering is that cock-ups are far more common than conspiracies. When you suspect your opponent of misbehaving you need to remember that it is much more likely it is their competence that is lacking, not their integrity.

The next point describes a response that is as bad as retaliation.

Don't be an appeaser

Although you should not retaliate, neither should you reward your opponent's outbursts with appeasement.

Don't blame your opponent

Blame is hardly ever received well. Blame invites defensiveness or retaliation. A classic example of how to avoid blaming someone would be to say 'I am upset', rather than 'you upset me'. If you want to criticise your opponent, then frame your comment as constructive criticism.

Don't disrespect your opponent

For example:

- 'You haven't done this very often have you?'
- 'Your company doesn't have a very impressive track record'
- 'If you had done your homework you would have known that ... '

Surely no experienced negotiator would utter such phrases ... wrong!

Don't be rude

Many of the comments in the previous point are pretty rude. So is talking over people. So is interrupting people. So is monopolising the conversation. So is boasting. So is patronising behaviour.

Don't cause your opponent to lose face

Don't criticise your opponent to their superiors. Don't boast about how good a deal you got after the deal is concluded. Your challenge is to ensure your opponent doesn't lose face whilst you walk away with the bigger slice of the cake.

Don't show deference to authority

If your opponent wheels in their boss or someone else senior from their organisation, don't be fooled into deferring to their authority.

Don't overuse a tactic

There are few things more irritating than negotiating with a 'one-trick pony'. If you continually issue threats, deliver ultimata, constantly refer to an absent third party or continually bluff, then you will probably lose the respect of your opponent.

Don't annoy your opponent

It is much easier to follow this advice if you are good at reading body language. It can be worth openly inviting your opponent to warn you if you are annoying them. The problem with annoyance is that your opponent may bottle it up, and the pressure may grow till they explode.

Don't offer a legal clause you wouldn't be willing to accept

I believe it is a mistake to use contract negotiations as an extension of bargaining, where you offer contractual clauses highly favourable to yourself in the expectation of being bargained down to something more reasonable. Life is too short for such silly games!

Summary

Bargaining is best treated as a game. This chapter has explained the principles the game is based on; the tactics to help you come out with a larger slice of the cake than your opponent; how to break a deadlock; and common mistakes and good practices.

One of the most satisfying parts of bargaining is when you manage to avoid bargaining becoming a zero-sum game. Finding things that cost the person offering them much less than their opponent values them, effectively conjures value out of thin air.

CHAPTER 6

Closure and commitment

Bargaining and haggling cannot go on for ever, and there comes the time when you must clinch the deal. The use of high-pressure closing techniques by unscrupulous salespeople is one reason why sales and negotiations have a somewhat tarnished image. This should not stop you using similar techniques in an ethical fashion.

There is a very simple closing technique that you will learn. If that doesn't work you are into the situation where you have to put your opponent under pressure.

Having closed the deal you must ensure that there is sufficient commitment from both sides to make sure the deal will last for a long time.

Simple closing

If you are in a buying situation then the simple close is:

IF you offer me one last compromise THEN I will do the deal.

If you are in a selling situation then the classic close is:

IF I offer you one last compromise THEN will you do the deal?

Obviously if you are buying you should always try to extract one last compromise in order to agree to close the deal. If you are selling, then an alternative closing technique is simply to ask for the deal, saying something like: 'I think I have exhausted what I can offer you. Will you do the deal?'

🔘 brilliant example

In one of the late Mark McCormack's books he tells an anecdote about a disastrous bargaining session in which he was accompanied by one of his youthful employees. In the bargaining session he could make no headway against a hostile client. He tells how he felt that the least he could do was show his apprentice that you should always ask for the deal. On being asked for the deal, the hostile client meekly agreed to buy!

You have to put your opponent under pressure

If the simple method doesn't work you are left with just two alternatives. Firstly, you can agree a rational process to break the deadlock, as I described in Chapter 5 on bargaining (arbitration; you divide I choose; toss a coin; meet in the middle; and the like). Secondly, you have to put your opponent under pressure.

Pressured closing

There are two ways to apply pressure: the first is to make threats and the second is to focus on the scarcity of some resource, such as time.

Making threats

I will start by repeating a piece of advice. Threats are best delivered unemotionally, in very polite language. For example, you might adopt a 'more in sorrow than in anger' style for a threat.

> threats are best delivered unemotionally

Some example threats:

- 'If you don't accept my offer then I'm afraid that I will be unable to do business with you.'
- 'Unless you make me an acceptable offer by (insert time) I'm afraid that I will be unable to do business with you.'
- 'Unless you reduce your price by £1,000 I think I'll have to see what your competitor can do.'
- 'Surely you don't want to lose the deal for £100?'

Applying pressure

The most common way to apply pressure is to focus on the scarcity of some resource. The most common resource to focus on is time.

You and your opponent may mutually agree to set a deadline by which time an agreement must be concluded. Alternatively you may unilaterally impose such a deadline, accompanied by a threat, either implied or explicit, that you will walk away if the deadline is not adhered to.

Some examples of other scarcity-based pressure tactics are:

- 'I can hold that price only until the end of the week.'
- 'Unless you agree to my price I won't be able to fit you into the diary and we won't be able to paint the outside of your house this summer.'
- 'I'll be able to put my best consultant on your job now, but I'll only reserve her for this work for another week, and if you haven't committed to fund the work by then you'll probably lose her.'
- 'I go on my summer vacation at the end of the week, so we need to get everything tied up before then.'
- 'The manufacturer changes its special offers each month so I can only honour this deal until the end of the week.'
- 'This item is very rare indeed, so if someone else buys it you will have a lot of trouble finding another.'
- 'There is just one in stock: once that is gone it will be months before I can get hold of another.'
- 'This is the last of the old stock, so I won't be able to get another.'
- 'The job offer is only valid for 30 days, after which we will offer the post to our second-choice candidate.'
- 'The manufacturer's annual price rise comes in at the end of the month.'

There is a narrow dividing line between acceptable pressure tactics and unethical ones. The following tactic is on the borderline of acceptability … partly because it is not credible. If the tactic was applied to a vulnerable person, most people would regard it as totally unacceptable.

When I phoned my manager he said I could offer you an extra £500 discount, but only if you can agree the deal today.

Assuming some of the tactics in this chapter have succeeded in closing the deal, how do you make it stick?

Commitment

Some deals are, by their nature, more solid than others. In England if you accept an offer on your house then it can be subject to renegotiation after

> some deals are more solid than others

the prospective purchaser has a building survey done. It is also not unusual for a purchaser to try to get a reduction in price just before contracts are exchanged. In such a situation there is really nothing the seller can do to make the deal more solid at the time they accept the initial offer. However, in many other situations there are practical measures that can be taken to make a deal more likely to stick, and to help a long-term relationship get off to a good start and last a long time.

When closing a deal, the sorts of closure that make the deal more likely to stick include:

- Signing a legal agreement
- Money changing hands, either for the full amount, a deposit or other form of advance payment
- Making a public announcement (e.g. a press release)
- Agreeing some positive follow-up action, such as a kick-off meeting.

If you can engineer the closure of your deal to include some items on this list then your deal is much more likely to hold up after the closure. Closing a deal is often the start of the next phase, and if that is the case you should always use the deal closure to agree the follow-up actions. If it is the start of an ongoing relationship you need to be sure you know who is leading that relationship from your side and start the relationship-building straight away. In short, you must maintain the momentum. It makes me weep to think of the number of times I have seen a deal closed and then it falls apart because one or both sides relax and don't follow up professionally.

brilliant tip

Draft a contract that will last the test of time. If you hope to have a long-term relationship with the other side (they are no longer your opponents now!) then you need to craft a contract that can last for years. For example, you need to think about clauses that allow renegotiation at points in the future. Few relationships remain static over a long period and trying to enforce contract conditions that are no longer appropriate to an evolving relationship is a recipe for disaster.

Summary

The simplest tactic for closing a deal is just to ask for it ... possibly with one last concession requested or offered. If asking for the deal does not work then you will have to increase the pressure on your opponent. You increase pressure either by politely making threats, or by focusing on the scarcity of some resource – most commonly time.

Once the deal is done, you must ensure that both sides are committed to the deal. Although closure is the end of negotiation, it is often the start of a new phase of cooperation. At the very least you must agree follow-up actions with the other side.

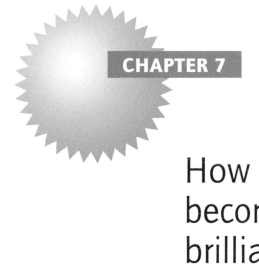

CHAPTER 7

How to become a brilliant negotiator

After the first edition of *Brilliant Negotiations* was published I got only one major suggestion for improvement. I received this suggestion many times, and it can be summed up by the question "I have read your book and understand what I am meant to do, but how do I get from my current skill level to become a brilliant negotiator?" I realised that this was a very good question, which I had not properly answered. This chapter answers this question.

To start I will summarise what are the essential qualities of a brilliant negotiator.

What makes you a brilliant negotiator?

Be tough – but not irritating or aggressive

A tough negotiator is someone who is determined to negotiate the best possible deal. A tough negotiator is someone who will walk away from a bad deal. Just as important as training yourself to be a tough negotiator is to also understand what a tough negotiator isn't:

- Don't be aggressive
- Don't get angry
- Don't shout
- Don't thump the table

- Don't irritate your opponent by overusing hardball negotiating tactics such as walk-outs, threats and ultimata.

Do your preparation/research properly

Knowledge really is power.

Read the situation – listen and watch!

The brilliant negotiator picks up on the verbal and non-verbal cues that the opponent sends deliberately and inadvertently.

Be creative

The brilliant negotiator spots those offers that cost you little to give, or cost your opponent little to give you. In this way the brilliant negotiator can exploit those situations where you can win something without your opponent losing.

Be charming … or at least polite

The most brilliant negotiators are both tough and charming. To a certain extent charm is a quality that only some people are blessed with. If you are not blessed with charm then being a good listener and being polite is a very good second best.

brilliant example

Joanna Lumley was both tough and charming when negotiating on behalf of the Gurkhas … Gordon Brown never stood a chance!

Be patient

Negotiators who are in a hurry tend to get worse deals than those who have patience.

Know when and how to close the deal

No matter how good you are at all the aspects of negotiations, you have to know when and how to secure the deal.

How do you become a brilliant negotiator?

You have already made a very good start ... you are reading this book. Someone who has read this book is much more likely to come away with a good deal than someone who hasn't. In addition, there are many good negotiation training courses available. However, there is no substitute for real-life experience ... so what do you do? At least negotiations are seldom a matter of life and death, so it is worth looking to a profession such as that of a surgeon to understand how you can improve your skills. A trainee surgeon will:

- Study the subject from books, lectures and videos before setting foot in an operating theatre
- Then be an observer in an operating theatre
- Then assist an experienced surgeon
- Tackle minor operations before major operations
- Have experienced back-up available the first time they do an operation.

There are obvious analogies for each of these steps for negotiators. Then, having become an experienced negotiator you need to keep your skills honed by constant practice.

One advantage a negotiator has that a surgeon doesn't is that they can practise at home. I strongly recommend that anyone who has to handle business negotiations should practise their negotiation skills at every opportunity in their home life.

brilliant tip

There is no doubt that a business negotiator becomes 'battle-hardened' when they negotiate regularly, and that a battle-hardened negotiator will outperform an opponent who in boxing parlance is 'ring rusty'. Many business negotiators do not do enough negotiating to become battle-hardened, and such people need to use negotiating opportunities in their home lives to keep their hand in.

Getting started

If you haven't haggled/bargained before then the best way to start is to say:

'What is your best offer/bid?'

Even people with a pathological fear of haggling can manage this, and it will get you a much better deal than paying the asking price, or accepting someone's first offer when you are selling.

The obvious place to go from this opening is to listen to the other person's offer/bid and come back with a counter-offer:

'If you could go to £X then we have a deal.'

You then are off into the negotiation.

Looking back at the start of this chapter there is a list of the qualities that distinguish a brilliant negotiator:

- Be tough – but not irritating or aggressive
- Do your preparation/research properly
- Read the situation – listen and watch!
- Be creative
- Be charming ... or at least polite

- Be patient
- Know when and how to close the deal.

We will now go through this list and see how an inexperienced negotiator can raise their game.

Toughening up

Of all the qualities of the brilliant negotiator, this is probably the most challenging. Many people see the pursuit of the best possible deal as a conflict, and a lot of people try to avoid conflict. To counter such thoughts you need to keep reminding yourself that almost everyone regards negotiations as a game, and provided you stick to the rules then very few of your opponents will think badly of you for fighting to get the best possible deal. Remember also that you will not be aggressive or rude, and will seldom use hardball tactics such as threats, ultimata and walk-outs.

brilliant tip

The best evidence that negotiating is a game is that almost everyone accepts that bluffing (a.k.a. lying) is acceptable.

brilliant tip

A smile on your face can not only make the whole experience more enjoyable, but will almost certainly lead to more money in your pocket at the end of the negotiation.

Even if you think you are being tough the chances are that you haven't set yourself high enough expectations about the deal you want. You need to experiment with just how far you can push your expectations. A good place to start is in negotiations within your home life, such as purchasing a car.

An excellent way to establish sensibly ambitious targets for your negotiations is to use Internet sites, discount outlets (such as car supermarkets), and auctions (physical and online). If you find face-to-face bargaining difficult, this approach will get you used to buying at bargain prices, and selling for top prices. Once you are used to buying low and selling high you will find it increasingly difficult to set yourself low expectations for face-to-face negotiations. In addition, using auctions regularly will teach you the benefits of discipline and patience.

brilliant tip

Don't believe people who say that you cannot act tougher than your personality allows. Very few people relish conflict, but almost everyone can conquer an innate fear of conflict.

A useful technique to use to help you toughen up is the third-party mandate – 'my wife/husband/partner/boss would never allow me to agree to that'. You can play the good cop, while blaming the third party (the bad cop) for stopping you from agreeing to a less than excellent deal.

If you are having trouble toughening up then ask a friend or colleague to negotiate for you … accompany them, but be careful not to undermine them. Seeing an experienced negotiator at work can inspire many inexperienced negotiators to set more challenging targets for a negotiation.

Preparation

Brilliant negotiators don't just think quickly on their feet, they are highly disciplined – and the most important aspect of discipline is to prepare carefully for a negotiation.

One side effect of doing preparation properly is that it will help an inexperienced negotiator overcome their nerves. Just like preparing for an exam, those who have done their revision properly will be more confident than those who haven't.

brilliant tip

Do not leave your preparation to the last minute. Many aspects of preparation, such as trying to get inside the head of your opponent, need days, not hours, of elapsed time to come to a considered opinion.

I would recommend flicking through the chapter on *Preparation* before a negotiation to quickly remind yourself of all the issues you need to consider or research before the negotiation begins.

Listen and watch

There are some useful techniques to use to improve your listening skills. The first is that you cannot listen when you are talking ... so talk less. Do not feel the need to fill a silence. You must remember that silence is quite likely to pressure your opponent into giving something away – be it information, or a better offer.

Another useful tactic is to take notes during a negotiation. This enforces a discipline on your listening, and will make you think about what your opponent has just said. It will also be a useful aide-memoire.

A third technique is to ask open questions, which will elicit useful information. 'What special offers are available at the moment?', 'what aspect of our product is most valuable to you?', etc. A related technique is to ask more detailed follow-up questions when your opponent make a general statement about something. If your opponent sends you a cue, you will usually want to probe your opponent about it in greater depth. In these ways you will develop a highly interactive discourse, which will be rich in information for you to listen to.

brilliant tip

Read a short book on body language. This should help you pick up more visual cues from your opponent.

Be creative

A creative offer is one which ensures that the negotiation isn't a zero-sum game. A zero-sum game is where one side can win something only if the other side loses something of the same absolute value. If one side can offer something that is worth much less to them than it is to their opponent, you can get an offer which is truly win/win. Many creative offers can be spotted during the preparation phase, and will be part of a good nego- tiator's armoury when the negotiation begins. Many creative opportunities are widely applicable, and so you will need to probe for issues such as delivery constraints, payment terms, etc. to see if the conditions are right for a creative offer. In addition, the good listener may spot other creative opportunities from what their opponent is saying.

Be polite

Remember that you can catch more flies with honey than with vinegar. One of the problems inexperienced negotiators face is that they tend to get anxious before a negotiation, so have lots of adrenalin in their blood stream. This leads to you talking too much, talking too loudly, and giving the appearance of being aggressive. There are lots of relaxation techniques you can prac-tise before a negotiation starts (such as breathing from your stomach/diaphragm) and these can be very helpful. You can also make a conscious effort to speak slower, speak less, and speak less loudly.

Probably the single best technique is to practise phrasing things in an unthreatening way. A classic example that is given in many books is to say 'I am upset', not 'you have upset me'. Also you can phrase strong statements almost apologetically: 'I am very sorry but there is no way my boss will let me agree to that.' A demand can always be phrased as a request: 'Would it be pos-sible for you to increase the discount from 10% to 20%?' When your opponent makes a concession you should express your gratitude. Always remember to say 'please' and 'thank you'.

Try to make yourself smile. Laugh at your opponent's jokes. Try to look as if you are enjoying yourself. This sort of behaviour will help you enjoy yourself.

brilliant tip

Someone who is both polite and a very good listener is 90% of the way to being charming.

There will be times when you have to have a row. If this happens you mustn't lose your temper because you must remain in control of yourself. Try not to shout, and don't make personal insults.

brilliant tip

If you are hosting the negotiation be generous with your hospitality, such as refreshments.

Be patient

After toughness, I think this is the hardest technique to master. Purchasing online and using online auctions is a good way of training yourself about the value of being patient. Remember it is a game and try not to get uptight and over-excited.

Know when and how to close the deal

The simplest way to know when to close the deal is when there are no subsidiary issues (such as product specification, delivery times, payment terms, etc.) left to settle. It is then time to propose a final offer on the main issue (such as the price). Chapter 6 on *Closure and commitment* tells you everything you need to know about how to close successfully. Flip through Chapter 6 before going into the negotiation.

The last sections in this chapter deal with two other techniques for improving your skills.

Experiment with new techniques

Don't just stick to a limited repertoire of negotiating techniques. Chapters 4 and 5 on *Haggling* and *Bargaining* describe a wealth of tried-and-tested stratagems. Try them out a few at a time to see which ones work well for you. Brilliant negotiators will be continually extending their abilities.

Analyse your performance

One of the best ways to improve your abilities is for you to hold a post mortem in your head after each negotiation. What worked well, and what didn't? With the benefit of hindsight, what would you have done differently? If someone else accompanied you in the negotiation, what did they feel you did well, and how do they think you could have done better?

Summary

The key qualities of a brilliant negotiator are:

- Be tough – but not irritating or aggressive
- Do your preparation/research properly
- Read the situation – listen and watch!
- Be creative
- Be charming … or at least polite
- Be patient
- Know when and how to close the deal.

Be tough – Remember that negotiations are a game. Keep setting yourself higher and higher expectations. Do not overuse hardball negotiating tactics and school yourself to speak slowly, not too loudly and not too much. Use Internet auctions, car supermarkets, discount websites, and the like to get yourself used to selling high and buying low – this will also teach you the value of patience.

Prepare properly – remember to allow yourself enough time to do your preparation thoroughly. Use your preparation to think of potentially creative offers.

Be polite – practise phrasing demands and threats in unaggressive language.

brilliant tips

Analyse your performance after a negotiation has finished, so you can see where you can improve.

Experiment with new negotiating techniques.

Flip through *Brilliant Negotiations* before a major negotiation.

CHAPTER 8

Negotiations masterclass

T his chapter contains the most probing questions about negotiations I have ever been asked. I will provide answers to some very important questions such as ethics, handling tough opponents, negotiating across a cultural divide and multi-party negotiations, to name but a few. It will give you the final touches you need to set you well on the way to becoming a brilliant negotiator.

What should you regard as unethical behaviour?

Certain behaviour is not just unethical, it can lead to your opponent successfully suing you or your organisation. If your opponent suffers damage because you deliberately misled them about a fact, and a court determines that a reasonable person could have reasonably relied on the misinformation you provided, then you are in danger of being successfully sued. For example, if you are selling a company, and you provide false accounts, then you will probably get into trouble (and so you should!). The only safe course of action is that if you get into any area where you think there is even a small chance that you could get sued, then don't do it.

What if you know something about the subject of the deal that your opponent would regard as significant – do you have a duty of disclosure? If a reasonable person would think you should disclose it, then you should. As an example, a reasonable person would probably think you should disclose a potential major fault in a car to a private buyer, but not if you are trading it in at a garage.

> ### brilliant tip
>
> Ethical behaviour is not just right, it is also good for business.

Are any tactics in this book unethical? The only tactic that you should consider avoiding for ethical reasons is nibbling – when you seek further concessions – after you have agreed a deal. Even this isn't black and white; it is just that if you are treating negotiations as a game, many people would think it is cheating.

What are the problems of negotiating with foreigners?

The reader will be aware that we live in an increasingly international, multi-cultural world. Ignoring such issues can lead you into a minefield of misunderstanding and unintentional offence. I deliberately framed this question using the emotive word 'foreigners' rather than a more politically correct phrase such as 'people from different cultures' to try to highlight the great problems that you may encounter dealing with people from different cultural backgrounds.

be sensitive about assuming that English will be used

The most extreme cultural difference is when you negotiate with someone who is not a native English speaker. If you are negotiating with an opponent who is not a native English speaker, then it is essential to be sensitive about assuming that English will be used in the negotiation. There are a number of techniques that can help:

● Always ask in advance if it is acceptable to use English. An apologetic explanation, such as the fact that you only speak

English, will often help. This is important because it will then be clear that you are not assuming that English is OK.

- If it is agreed that English will be used, ask how fluently your opponent speaks English, and ensure that you converse with them in a way that is appropriate to their fluency in English. This will show that you are both professional and polite.

- You will need to speak slowly and clearly, avoiding colloquialisms. Use short sentences and try not to use different words to describe the same thing.

- Humour often does not cross the language divide and is usually best avoided.

- If possible, include a supporting member of your negotiating team who is a native speaker of the non-English language. They can make introductions in the native language, speak rapidly in the native language and act as interpreter, if necessary. They can also help smooth over any cultural gaffes you may make.

- An area that is a particular minefield is whether you should learn enough of the foreign language to say 'good morning', 'please' and 'thank you'. Similarly, should you bow in Japan? You should seek local advice in each and every case.

Even if you are talking to another English-speaking culture you should be aware that many words will have different meanings, possibly different pronunciations, and that many colloquialisms will not be understood. Again, humour often does not cross a cultural divide and is usually best avoided.

Cultural differences can also be a major source of problems. At a superficial level, the world is becoming more homogeneous and Westernised,

> do not let this superficial similarity fool you

with many aspects of American culture spreading to other countries. Do not let this superficial similarity between countries fool you into ignoring the deep differences between different cultures and the way they conduct business. The list of areas in which it is very easy to cause offence includes:

- What is considered polite and what is considered rude
- What is considered respectful and disrespectful
- What is considered offensive behaviour
- Attitudes to personal space (how close it is acceptable to physically approach or touch someone)
- How meetings are handled (e.g. the Japanese approach to a first meeting is very different from other cultures, and as a consequence the Japanese tend to have a very slow and formal approach to starting The Sharing)
- Acceptability of some business practices (e.g. some cultures find acceptable what other cultures would regard as dishonest)
- Personal habits
- Attitudes to women
- Eating conventions
- Religious issues
- Attitude to alcohol consumption in social settings
- Body language
- The giving and receiving of presents.

The best thing you can do is to find someone in your organisation from the culture you are dealing with, and get them to brief you on the cultural issues. It is also well worth trying to get someone from the local culture to act as your second in the negotiation.

What do you do if you come up against an opponent as tough, or tougher, than you?

You have to accept that this negotiation will produce a much more balanced deal than you are used to getting with more accommodating opponents. It may be worth openly discussing the issue with your opponent, especially if they are showing signs of frustration that their usual tactics are not

tough negotiators get very accustomed to getting good deals

working. There are so few really tough negotiators around that the tough negotiators get very accustomed to getting good deals.

This is a situation where you have to keep a rational eye on your walk-away scenario. Don't reject a deal that is better than your walk-away scenario just because you are annoyed that you aren't getting as good a deal as usual.

Using shock tactics can sometimes work. Walking out in a simulated rage can help convince your opponent that you really will not back down all the time.

Shock tactics can sometimes work

Is there a good time to make an offer?

It is common for your opponent's concentration levels to be high at the start of a negotiating session, to dip in the middle of the session, and then to come back up again as the session nears its close. If you engineer a time out in the middle of a session then your opponent's concentration level will be high when you come back together after the time out. Offers tend to be best received when your opponent's concentration levels are high.

brilliant tip

Outside of your business life, ignore the advice in this book if you want to. You have a duty to get the best deal for your organisation. However, in your personal life it is up to you to decide how tough you want to negotiate.

What is the worst mistake you can make?

I would single out the negotiator who makes a deal that they should have walked away from. In a business context the costs to a firm, in terms of money, staff morale, lost opportunities, and the like, of a really bad deal can be very severe indeed.

On a personal level, buying the wrong item can be expensive, inconvenient and a constant source of annoyance. Choosing the wrong tradesperson because you chased the lowest price can have water coming through the roof, cracks in the walls, and the like.

Name three other very bad mistakes a negotiator can make

The reader will not be surprised that top of my list is not being tough enough. I don't really think I need say any more on this subject.

A negotiator who doesn't listen intently to their opponent is making one of the worst, most fundamental mistakes in the book. If you cannot read the cues your opponent is sending you then you are going to get a far from optimal deal.

Displaying bad manners rounds off the list of three. Good manners cost you nothing, but are key to making a great deal. Tough but polite is a

good manners cost you nothing

very good way of getting a great deal. Weak, rude and deaf is the perfect cocktail to rob you of a brilliant deal.

What are the three easiest mistakes to make?

1 Failing to do your preparation properly

Brilliant negotiators will nearly always be very busy people. Busy people will often fail to find the time to do proper research and planning before going into a negotiation. One of the problems with the preparation phase is that you cannot just sit down and blitz it all in a couple of hours. One of the most important aspects of preparation for a major set-piece negotiation is to talk to all the major stakeholders and ensure you understand their key concerns. Major stakeholders are likely to be very busy people and hence difficult to pin down quickly, so you must plan to meet them some time in advance of The Sharing.

2 Getting emotional and possibly losing your temper

Even brilliant negotiators are human, so may well forget to act like Mr Spock in *Star Trek*. Even experienced negotiators will get tense and charged with adrenalin before face-to-face negotiations, so you have the perfect setting for an emotional outburst.

3 Becoming too emotionally committed to the object of the negotiation, or too committed to doing the deal

Doing a deal you should have walked away from is the single most serious mistake you can make, so you will see why this is such a dangerous, easy mistake to make.

What is the hardest aspect of negotiations?

Keeping a grip on the financial implications of a deal is very difficult indeed. Even if you seek advice from experts in your organisation you will often find it very hard to get straight answers. As an example, if you offer an extended warranty for a product or service, how much have you given away? The safest course is to be pessimistic about financial estimates so that if you do a deal then it is unlikely to be worse than your walk-away scenario.

What do you do if you come up against an inexperienced negotiator or inexperienced organisation?

Such negotiations tend to last much longer than they would if the other side is experienced. When both sides are experienced they will both know the standard solutions to standard problems, and will understand how negotiators normally behave in that area of business.

You may be lucky and be able to direct your opponent to some standard source of advice. For example, a new author can join the Society of Authors that publishes lots of pamphlets and will advise you on your contract. Also a new author can buy a book such as Rachael Stock's *The Insider's Guide to Getting Your Book Published* (White Ladder Press). It is worth having a source of useful Internet resources that will help your opponent get up to speed on your business area. Whatever you do, don't recommend that they read *Brilliant Negotiations* – you can direct them to almost any other best-selling title to help them become a better informed but not very tough negotiator.

be scrupulously honest when guiding them

In such situations you can tell your opponent that they will have to trust you when you advise them on standard practice, and you must then be scrupulously honest when guiding them.

You receive insider information, what do you do?

Using some sorts of insider information is illegal, and obviously you should try to avoid receiving such information. If you are required to notify the authorities that you have it, then do so; otherwise do not consciously use it.

If there are no legal barriers then you are free to use it. You may need to be discreet to protect your source, but that is the only limitation you face.

Remember that you need to avoid putting your opponent in this situation, so make sure you are discreet about what you say in the bar, toilets, etc., to ensure you do not inadvertently leak information to the opposition.

What do you do if you just cannot force yourself to be a tough negotiator?

In your personal life, the obvious answer is to get a friend or relation to handle the negotiation for you. In a business situation, you need to get a colleague, or a professional negotiator, to lead the negotiation.

The very least you should do is ask: 'What is your best price/offer?'

Are there times when you should avoid being a negotiator?

In certain situations it is usual to use a professional, such as a barrister or solicitor, to negotiate for you. At other times you may have paid for such a service, for example through your trades union membership or through an insurance policy. There are three potential advantages to using a professional:

1   They may be more experienced as a negotiator.

2 They may have much more knowledge about relevant information such as case law.

3 If you are emotionally involved (e.g. if you have just been fired or disciplined) they may be more effective because they can be dispassionate.

Should you treat loved ones and friends the same as everyone else?

You have to ask yourself if the importance of love and friendship overrides the desire to get a good deal ... for me, it does.

What do you do if your opponent has only limited authority to negotiate?

In a few circumstances you may be able to demand to negotiate with someone who has more authority to close a deal; however, in most circumstances, you will not be able to change your opponent. Knowing that you will probably be subject to delay and nibbling you may decide to exercise your walk-away scenario ... but usually you will want the deal badly enough to stay put. So what do you do? The best technique is to apply the tactic of reciprocity. Tell your opponent that you are in the same situation: so, for example, when they nibble, you nibble back.

> you will seldom be able to change your opponent

Can you use a tactic that is at odds with your personality?

This is usually used as an excuse for not doing something that you find difficult. Many aspects of professional life are difficult, for example, few managers relish confronting staff who are underperforming or guilty of misconduct. Management and negotiations are about doing the right thing regardless of whether you find them unpleasant. In a business context you are paid to behave like a professional negotiator, so stop moaning

and get on with it. In your personal life you don't have to negotiate in a way you don't want to, just don't complain when you
don't get a very good deal.

What do you do if your opponent tries not to be as open as you during The Sharing?

Sadly a number of negotiation courses and books recommend
that you try to discover more information than you offer in The
Sharing. If you come up against someone like this, then you
should openly request a reciprocal approach to information
sharing. If they continue to behave competitively, then you have
to apply the tactic of reciprocity and play them at their own
game.

How do you handle a walk-out?

The best way to handle a walk-out is to wait for the other side
to contact you, or wait a significant length of time before con-
tacting them. Being impatient is playing into their hands.

When a negotiation resumes after a walk-out, this can be a very
good time to make an imaginative 'out of the box' offer. It is also
worth remembering to act perfectly normally – almost as if they
hadn't walked out at all.

How do you handle a threat?

There is no simple answer to this question because each situation must be judged according to its unique circumstances. Do
whatever you think is likely to get you the best result: the only
thing that is definitely wrong is to allow your annoyance to affect
your decision. If the other side has the leverage and you giving
in (at least partially) to a threat will
lead you to a deal that is better than   **do not let pride hold**
your walk-away scenario, then do   **you back**
not let pride hold you back.

Can you negotiate with someone who shows they have no integrity?

Yes. What do you do about it? I suggest you adopt an appropriate form of defensive negotiations, where your approach is based on your knowledge that your opponent may behave badly. If you intend to build a long-term relationship with the other side, you will again have to be prepared to defend yourself against the potential for despicable behaviour. You may be in such a powerful position you have the luxury of refusing to deal with such people and organisations, but most negotiators just have to cope.

The same answer applies to the question as to whether you can negotiate with someone whom you do not trust.

CHAPTER 9

Knowing it,
doing it,
saying it

This chapter illustrates the techniques described in this book, by taking some common negotiating scenarios and discussing how you might tackle them. Only by considering real-life scenarios will the value of the techniques described here be fully revealed. In addition, these scenarios are important situations which you may well be able to exploit in your personal and professional lives.

Negotiating a pay rise

Preparation

If your organisation has an annual pay round, you shouldn't leave your preparations until the time for pay rise decisions is bearing down on you. You should start thinking about your next pay rise as soon as the last pay round has finished.

You should do the following research, analysis and groundwork.

Understand how your organisation's reward system works
Time and again I have seen people complaining about their pay rise in terms that offer their boss no help at all in justifying a pay increase within the constraints of their organisation's reward system.

If your organisation's pay system sets pay based on a number of factors of which the only two variables that you can influence are your overall performance assessment and your grade, you need to concentrate all your efforts on getting the best possible performance assessment, and planning your next promotion. In addition, if you are cunning, you can negotiate for non-pay-based rewards, such as support to get a qualification that would improve your employability and also be a motivating experience.

who is it important to impress?

Many organisations try to tie the pay rise offered to your level of performance. If your annual performance assessment is very important, you need to understand how that assessment is made. Who is it important to impress, and what will impress them?

Understand how you are valued by your boss and your organisation

The first thing to get out of your head is all your thoughts about how you think you should be valued. You need to understand how the organisation actually values you because that is the reality you have to deal with.

Although every organisation will have different mechanisms, I can give three very useful pointers:

- The more difficult you are to replace and the more damage your leaving will cause, the more highly you will be valued.
- The more likely you are to leave, the more highly you will be valued.
- The higher maintenance you are, the less the organisation will value you. High-maintenance people are those who

require more management effort because they complain, are disruptive, are difficult to find work for, need supervision, cannot be trusted not to put their foot in it, require cover because they take lots of sick leave, and the like.

Assess your leverage

If your boss perceives that there is little or no chance that you will leave, you have very little leverage. You need to do and say things that increase the perception that you might leave. There are subtle ways of creating this perception and unless you are prepared to back up a threat to leave, you should stick with the subtle approach. The sorts of hints that you can drop include:

- Changes in your personal circumstances that might cause you to re-evaluate your career, for example, getting married or having a baby
- A long commute to work
- Demonstrating an awareness of what is going on in the jobs market
- Shortage of money (but not because you are bad at managing your personal finances)
- Saving up for something such as a house or a flat.

Much weaker than the perception that you might leave, but important nonetheless, is to stress that a decent pay rise is essential to maintaining your morale. Many organisations will know that poor pay rises can be a major demotivator. If you cannot aspire to a good pay rise, then you will need to use the motivational argument as the main reason why you shouldn't be given a poor pay rise.

> stress that a decent pay rise is essential to maintaining your morale

Use a performance or career management system

You should use a performance management or career management system as part of your preparations for the next pay round.

You should ask questions that make your case for good pay rises in future.

brilliant question

'What can I do that would make me more valuable to the organisation?' This question has two good effects. The answer you get will let you know how you can increase your value to the organisation, which may well eventually translate into earning more money. Secondly, it shows that you care about being valuable, and people who want to be valued highly will be identified as people with significant pay aspirations.

Assess your attitude to risk

You must realise that the more you are paid the more an organisation will expect from you, and the greater the danger that at some time in the future your services may no longer be required. It is well worth fighting hard to be paid your market value, but you should seriously consider moderating your demands to ensure you are not overpaid.

Identify your market value

In certain circumstances this will be a very important piece of information – particularly if you are negotiating the pay for a new job. An awareness of what you could get outside your organisation will affect the credibility of any threat (implied or explicit) that you may leave. Job advertisements are a ready source of such information, although your organisation will know that these represent an optimistic assessment of what you might earn.

Assess your pay relative to your peers'

Managers usually know that internal relativities are a greater source of dissatisfaction than pay being out of line with outside pay levels. This means that knowing how your pay compares to your peers' is important to assess your realistic aspirations. Some organisations try to keep everyone's pay secret, but even in such organisations information tends to leak out.

Identify rewards other than pay

In many organisations you do not get much chance to negotiate a pay rise, all you can do is to prepare the ground so that you are likely to be offered a decent rise. Many organisations have a 'take it, or leave it' attitude ... or maybe that should be a 'take it, or leave us' attitude. If you work for such an organisation you may find that your boss is much more susceptible to you bargaining that you want something other than an increase in your headline pay. Examples include:

- eligibility for an allowance (e.g. a car allowance)
- a perk (e.g. medical insurance, or a company car)
- getting on a training course or some other form of career development
- permission to work on a particular project
- some additional flexibility in your work patterns
- more annual leave (either a one-off or an increase in your annual allowance).

The Sharing

If you are negotiating for a new job then you need to do all the relationship building, exchanging your frames for the negotiation, and the like, that Chapter 3 on The Sharing discusses in detail.

When you are negotiating with your current employer, many of the techniques of The Sharing are not needed. Your main objective in The

find out how much leverage you have

Sharing is to find out how much leverage you have ... before you make a fool of yourself (at best) or you talk yourself out of a job (at worst). Go in with a fairly demanding demeanour and you will not need a degree in body language to know if you have little leverage. You will then go into the bargaining phase with sensible aspirations.

Bargaining

Consider the following three scenarios:

1   The annual pay round

2   A new job

3   You tell your employer that you have another job offer.

The annual pay round

In many cases you will not be permitted to negotiate, in which case you need to prepare the ground well during the preceding year, and if you really cannot accept the pay rise then look for another job.

If you get an annual review, you can use it to conduct a pseudo bargaining session. Many of the sorts of arguments you can deploy have already been introduced:

- I really want to stay but I am having to think about leaving because ...
- If I left, you would have problems because ...
- The sorts of offer I will get outside are ...

Then put your boss on the spot by directly asking what sort of pay rise is being considered. Even if you get a hand-waving answer you will have made the point that you care deeply about your pay. If you get a more precise answer then you will probably want to express disappointment with any figures mentioned, except if the sums quoted delight you, when you should say that you are pleased.

A new job

You are now bargaining with a potential new employer. There is a paradox that you will face in that the less you want the job the more pay you will be able to get.

brilliant example

When I was in my late 20s I applied for a job in the Electronic Computer Aided Design business. I went for an interview and came to the conclusion (correctly as it turned out) that the company had no long-term future. Consequently I turned down its first offer ... and then its second offer, and finally on getting the third offer, I explained why I wouldn't be joining. If I had really wanted the job, I would never have had the nerve to play 'chicken' so aggressively.

You tell your employer that you have another job offer

If you wish to use a job offer to negotiate a new salary then you need to tell your employer what you have been offered. You should tell the truth, but not necessarily the whole truth. For example, if the pension in your new job is less attractive, or more expensive, then you need not admit this. Then invite your current employer to make you an offer to stay, or if you know what your walk-away point is you may choose to reveal it. There is little harm in playing 'chicken' because you can probably backtrack and accept the last offer. I have heard employers threaten their employees with the fact that if they continue to play hardball they may damage their relationship with their current employer ... this is usually untrue.

> you can probably backtrack and accept the last offer

The sales negotiator

I stressed earlier in this book that ideally when selling a product or service, one wants to complete the sale before starting the negotiations. I suspect when I wrote that a number of readers shouted: 'But there's only one of me!' This example discusses some of the issues when the salesperson and negotiator are one and the same person.

Preparation

One thing that distinguishes the brilliant salesperson/negotiator from the rest is a total understanding and passion for the product or service. In particular, what are the key differentiators between the product/service and the competition? You also need to be up to date on prices, special offers, delivery times, and the like.

You need to know all you can about the prospective customer. Even if the initial contact was a telephone enquiry you need to capture any intelligence the customer lets drop. If you take the call yourself, or can control the people who may take the call, try to capture three key pieces of information:

1   How did you hear about our product or service? This is not only valuable information on the effectiveness of your organisation's marketing, it can give the salesperson/ negotiator vital intelligence. Is it repeat custom? Did the potential customer have a personal recommendation? Did the customer read a special offer? Did they read a piece of PR planted in the press?

2   What product or service are you interested in?

3   Why are you interested in the product or service? If you can find out anything about the motivation for the purchase then this will help the salesperson/negotiator.

brilliant example

A customer phones a roofing company about a leaking flat roof and says that water is coming into their dining room. When the salesman turns up he should know that it is likely the customer wants to get the problem fixed quickly.

The Sharing

Listening is an essential technique for the negotiator, and it is as important for a salesperson. You can sell someone only something that they want to buy, so listen hard to what the customer wants. Also listen hard for any cues the potential customer is sending you. The brilliant salesperson/negotiator will be looking for buying signals that are not price-related.

brilliant example

If a customer mentions that they have been let down by a previous supplier, they are sending a strong cue that they want to buy from a more reliable supplier this time. The salesperson should give customer references and supply any other information that shows how confident the customer can be that they will not have another bad experience.

Bargaining phase

If you are a salesperson as well as a negotiator, you need to remember that lowering the price is likely to be a much less powerful way to close a deal than you might imagine. It is very important you find the non-price differentiators and focus on them.

Negotiating a contract

If you are involved in a set-piece commercial negotiation then you need to understand the contractual terms being negotiated. If you are not experienced in contracts then there are three ways to improve your knowledge:

1   Read a book. There are plenty of simple guides to contract law, so buy one and read it.

2   Use the Internet. If you put the two search words *understanding* and *contracts* into a search engine, you will get many really useful resources on the first half a dozen pages of results. You can then refine your search to the particular sort of contract you are negotiating. In addition, there are a number of cheap subscription services to help you – just look at the sponsored links.

3   If you have a contract lawyer on tap, get them to give you an existing, similar contract. Read it through a number of times, and then sit down with your lawyer for an hour and get them to explain any bits you don't understand. You will easily find dictionaries of legal definitions on the Internet to help you with that strange language called *legalese*.

avoid using the drafting of the contract as an additional weapon

Try to avoid using the drafting of the contract as an additional weapon in your negotiating armoury. Agree the terms with your opponent and then have fair and equitable contract clauses drawn up that implement those terms.

Settling a dispute with a neighbour

This is an interesting example because it may have little or nothing to do with money.

Preparation

It is essential, but often very time-consuming, to write down a precise chronology of events pertinent to the dispute. Get all your evidence (letters, etc.) together and neatly file it. If the dispute could end up in court, then research the law and case law relevant to your situation. You can use the Internet, talk to a lawyer, or bodies such as a Citizen's Advice Bureau, a trade body, and the like. Even if you hope to avoid going to court, the strength of your legal position is key to assessing your leverage.

You need to work out what sort of negotiated deal you would find acceptable. You must try hard to be realistic as your emotions are probably running high. Seek advice from friends, family and other advisers about what is reasonable to expect.

Find out what you can about your neighbour, so you know what you are up against. If, for example, the neighbour is a serial litigator then you need to know.

What is your walk-away scenario? Again you need to be realistic … for example, is it really sensible to pursue your neighbour through the courts?

The Sharing

The first question to ask yourself is whether you wish to meet your neighbour face-to-face or whether it might be better to meet with a conciliator present.

> it might be better to meet with a conciliator present

You must find out whether there is a dispute over the facts, or whether the facts are agreed and the dispute is over what to do about an agreed situation. While you are doing this, and all other aspects of The Sharing, … **keep your cool**.

If you think you have some strong legal cards in your hand, then you may well want to lay those cards on the table. Your neighbour may then want to explain what they think the legal situation is.

You will need to share the key issues that both sides want to get out of the negotiation. Don't assume that this is obvious: you should both probe deeply as to what the real issues underlying the dispute are. For example, if the dispute is over noise:

● Is it the level of the noise?

● Is it the times the noise occurs?

● Is it the frequency of the noise?

● Is it the response to requests to turn the noise down?

A key issue to discover is whether your neighbour wants to resolve the situation amicably. Hopefully both sides want an amicable settlement and you can move to the bargaining phase.

Bargaining phase

You need to agree with your neighbour whether you want to bargain face-to-face or whether you prefer to agree on an arbitrator, or take the dispute to a court.

The key weapons at your disposal are:

● Logical arguments

● If we ended up in court then the court would probably say that ...

● A reasonable person would say that ...

● If you could address these particular issues then that would go a long way to resolving the dispute.

Stay calm, listen for cues, ask questions, be flexible; in other words, remember to use all the standard bargaining techniques. However, this is a good time to ignore my advice to be a tough negotiator. If ever there is a time for win/win, this is it.

if ever there is a time for win/win, this is it

brilliant example

If you are dealing with trespass from school children you can mention to the school your concern over your legal liability if a child hurts themselves climbing into your garden, or falling into your pond.

Buying a house

This, and its partner section *Selling your house*, discuss the most significant transactions that most people undertake. Although I strongly recommend that you treat negotiations as a game, few people can manage this trick when buying or selling a house. The stakes are too high, and the standards of behaviour of many people you will deal with are so low – lying, deceit and dishonourable behaviour are so common that the experience is seldom pleasant. There are, however, some general truths that everyone needs to be aware of.

Most people will still deal with traditional estate agents, so it is important to understand what motivates them. When valuing a house they are motivated to over-value in order to secure the vendor as a client. When selling a house they are motivated to get the vendor to accept a low offer because it loses them only a small amount of commission, but guarantees a cheap, quick sale ... and hence a cheap, quick chance to bill the vendor for the commission.

Solicitors get (well) paid even if they aren't very efficient. Solicitors get paid even if a sale falls through – in fact, they will probably make more money in such a situation. Like surveyors they are very interested in never offering advice that could get them sued, so they are unlikely to understate any legal problems. As a consequence, solicitors can sometimes appear to be the cause of sales falling through. This means that it is well worth finding a really good solicitor. Remember it is the person, not the firm, who is important. As is so often the case, a personal recommendation is the best way to find a good solicitor. Always check fees upfront, and think whether you want to ask for a fixed-price quotation. Some solicitors will even negotiate on price ... so give it a try.

brilliant tip

Buyers and sellers need to nag their solicitors constantly to act quickly. The longer a sale drags on, the greater the chance for something to go wrong.

Surveyors employed by mortgage providers are primarily interested in ensuring that the mortgage provider's money is safe. Their second interest is ensuring that they cannot be sued for missing faults in a house.

Preparation

Make sure you can get a mortgage before going any further. Think carefully about the best type of mortgage for you, and remember that interest rates can rise fast. Also remember that many mortgage sellers earn large commissions from sales of certain products, and hence push such products hard. When working out your budget, don't forget solicitor's fees, stamp duty, removal expenses, etc. Work on the basis that you may have to accept a lower price for any house you have to sell. Having checked your financial position, work out what your budget is. I recommend not pushing your budget to the limit, but allow for the possibility of future illness or redundancy. As a minimum, you need savings that will allow you to pay your mortgage for a year. Then view as many houses in and around your price range as possible. Once you have viewed a range of houses you will get a very good idea about prices – so when you find a house you are interested in, you will know whether it is over-priced.

I recommend that you decide the extent to which your house is an investment, or whether you are mainly interested in buying a home. This will determine how aggressive you are willing to be in negotiating the price.

If you are buying a new house, especially one that isn't yet complete, or one on a development that is in progress, then you may have problems if the developer goes out of business, or decides to cease building. Also remember that some developments may suffer in later years from problems such as subsidence or poor sewerage systems.

If you are buying abroad, be careful to do full research about any local problems you may encounter.

brilliant tip

If you are buying a house in an area you are not very familiar with then you need to spend as long as possible in the area so you understand the local market, such as which are the desirable and less desirable areas.

brilliant tip

Don't get too fixed about what features a house must have. Many people end up buying a property that is a long way from their ideal initial specification.

brilliant tip

In a buyers' market, it is the very desirable properties that tend to sell best. As a consequence, when buying it is often worth paying the premium for a house in a good area, or one which has a 'wow' factor.

Decide if you can realistically invest the time, money and effort in a property that needs a lot of work. It is usually more cost effective to buy a property that is in good decorative order, where the kitchen and bathrooms do not need replacing.

The Sharing

When viewing a house always be polite about the property. Do not run a property down to its owners in the mistaken belief that this will help you in a negotiation. Most owners want to sell to people they like.

Ask the owners what their situation is about moving out. How keen are they to sell? The keener they are to sell, the better the chances are that your purchase will proceed quickly.

Haggling

You need to take account of the state of the housing market. If it is a buyers' market then you need to take advantage of it. If it is a sellers' market then you need to try to appear an attractive buyer. In a sellers' market, a good offer from a buyer with a long purchasing chain is very unlikely to be attractive to a vendor.

The first and most important issue about your proposed purchase is how long the property has been on the market. If it has been on the market for a long time it was probably initially over-priced either because of over-optimism, or because the owners didn't fully allow for some innate problems with the property (such as noise), so you should aim to negotiate a significant reduction in the price. Secondly, find out if the owners have somewhere else to go, or whether the house has vacant possession, or failing this, are the owners willing to move out into rented accommodation? Long chains are very bad news when buying or selling houses.

You are then into a classic haggling situation, but your preparation will let you know what the house is worth. This is particularly important if a house has only recently been put on the market. Remember that if you are bidding to an estate agent, they will initially try to get you to raise your offer, but if you are the only person interested they will probably be trying to get the vendor to accept your offer. If there are competing offers the estate agent will probably favour the offer with the shortest chain.

brilliant tip

One of the best ways to get a bargain is to sell your house first and move into rented accommodation. You are then a first-time buyer.

Arrange an independent survey as soon as possible. Get a recommendation of a good independent surveyor. If the survey finds any costly problems, then it is perfectly acceptable to renegotiate the price.

Demanding a price reduction just before contracts are signed is unfortunately not unknown. I hope you aren't the sort of person to try this. If you don't intend to use this underhand tactic then mention it during the initial negotiations, as it may help you get your offer accepted.

Selling your house

Preparation

Ideally you have been checking house prices in your local paper over the time you have lived in your home, so you will know how your type of house in your area compares to similar houses in other areas. A careful examination of house prices in your local paper(s) will give you a ballpark estimate of your home's value. Even if you intend to sell privately, or via the Internet, I suggest getting valuations from three reputable local estate agents. Personal recommendation is the best way to locate good estate agents. When having your house valued, ask the valuer to give you the price for a quick sale.

brilliant tip

Very few houses sell for more than they are worth. If a house doesn't sell quickly, the vendor often ends up having to accept less than if they had priced their house competitively in the first place. If you price very competitively, you will sometimes get lots of interest and you may get a price above what you asked.

Negotiate hard to get the lowest possible commission rate from the estate agent. Only offer exclusivity to an agent for a fixed period. If they know you are pricing your house competitively, they will be keen to get your business because they know they have a good chance of securing a quick sale.

Consider how you can shorten the sales chain; especially consider your willingness to move out into rented accommodation.

If you have selected an estate agent then insist on reviewing their brochure before it is printed or put on the Internet. You may well find crucial errors and omissions.

The Sharing

If possible, show potential buyers around the house yourself. Don't oversell your house, but mention good aspects that aren't in the brochure. Ask potential buyers how quickly they will be in a position to sign contracts. If you are able to move out when they need to move in, then be sure to mention this fact. You need to form an assessment as to whether the buyers are trustworthy people.

Haggling

If you have priced competitively then make it clear the house is already a bargain. If you have overpriced then you need to be willing to move towards a more realistic price. Remember that a buyer who can sign contracts quickly is worth their weight in gold. If it subsequently turns out that they cannot sign contracts quickly, you should either put the house back on the market or renegotiate the price.

If your buyer tries to negotiate a last-minute reduction in price, you have to decide if you are going to make a principled stand and invite them to take a long walk off a short pier ... after all, they stand to lose all their costs, too. Another approach is to offer them a small reduction in price. Any other course of action I leave in your hands.

Buying a new washing machine, fridge, dishwasher, etc.

Preparation

Often the most important thing you have to do is work out what is the right product for your needs. Then ensure you buy from a competitively priced source. Remember that many such purchases involve taking away your old appliance and installing the new one – remember to factor in these costs.

The Sharing

Here is where you can get expert advice about what you might buy. If the advice is indeed expert, then after-sales service is likely to be good, too.

Haggling

Local suppliers can often be competitive with national chains and the Internet ... if you push them on price. They are also likely to be able to offer good service on removing old appliances and installing new ones. You also have a local contact for any after-sales problems. In addition, the situation with local suppliers is 'use them, or lose them'.

Having building works done

This is an interesting example because managing risk is probably the dominant issue. The safest approach is to get a good architect to draw up detailed plans for you. This will help you get the best possible design, and also allows you to get three fixed-price quotations from reputable builders. A good architect will be able to give you a ballpark figure for the work. Make sure you get personal recommendations for the three bidders. Read the detail of the quotes very carefully, and decide which quote you like best (which may well not be the cheapest). Having selected the winning bid, you can have a bargaining session to try to get a little bit more for your money, but don't be too tough – you have to give the builder a sensible profit margin or corners will be cut in the building work.

If your project is over £30K I would definitely recommend the approach outlined above. For smaller jobs, you may still get an architect involved, or you can talk your requirements over with three builders and get them to draw up detailed quotes.

An alternative approach is to develop a relationship with a trusted builder and let them work on a time-and-materials basis. You will be taking a greater risk, but I know a number of people who have used this approach successfully. It is also a good approach to very risky jobs, where many builders will be reluctant to quote.

🔘 brilliant example

I was having work done on a first-floor walkway, and a large section of wrought iron railings had to be lifted up by 15cm. No-one would quote, so I contacted the metal working firm with the best reputation in the area and asked them to do the job on a time-and-materials basis. They did an excellent job for a reasonable price.

Having double glazing, conservatory, kitchen or bathroom fitted

Preparation

You need to decide whether you are buying the fittings and doing it yourself (possibly with help from sub-contractors), or buying the bits and having them fitted by a local fitter, or using a local or national company to do the whole job.

☀ brilliant tip

If you are using a national company or a large/medium-sized local company, then insist on their best fitters working for you. If they just say all their fitters are good, then go elsewhere.

The Sharing

Here is where you get advice on how best to do the job. If a company or independent fitter offers good advice then it is likely they take customer service seriously.

> **✦ brilliant tip**
>
> If you spend a small fortune on a house improvement it is unlikely
> to increase the resale price of your house much more than a
> modestly priced version of the same improvement.

Haggling

National firms often start with fake offers and fake haggling
– starting from a ludicrously high figure. Always get multiple
quotes and the national firms will usually come down close to
the price of local firms.

Having a new boiler fitted

This is another example where risk management is a key issue.
Do you go to a small local supplier, a larger local supplier or a
national company? Each has obvious pros and cons as far as risk
is concerned. I recommend getting three quotes from suppliers
with good reputations. Read the quotes very carefully and accept
the one you find most attractive. You should query the bidders
if they are offering anything out of the ordinary. Having selected
your favourite quotation, you may be able to negotiate a slightly
better deal.

If you are under tight time pressures, you will want to check when
they could do the work before selecting a bidder. Alternatively
you may have a trusted supplier and will go straight to them
because you are confident of prompt, good service.

Renewing your insurance, energy supplier, car
breakdown cover, etc.

Loyalty will cost you dear. Every year you should get a new/
better quotation from an alternate supplier. You can then tell

your current provider about the new quote and they will almost certainly match it. Alternatively, you can punish them by changing provider.

Buying a new/used car

Preparation

There are a lot of questions you need to answer before you go in search of a new or used car. The first thing to do is to try to write down and answer that list of questions. To help you I will list just some of the common questions:

- Is now really the right time to change your car?
- How much can you afford to pay, and how will you finance the purchase?
- Do you have a preference between buying new, ex-demonstrator or used?
- What is your appetite for risk? Are you willing to buy at auction, or from a private individual? Is the quality and length of warranty an important issue?
- What sort of car do you want in terms of body style, size, performance, fuel type, fuel economy, VED band, insurance group, number of seats, etc.?
- Are there mandatory features you must have, such as air conditioning, a spare wheel, a hatchback, etc.?
- Are there any features you will not tolerate, such as an electric handbrake?
- Are you willing to sell your old car privately or at auction, or via one of the reputable websites that buy cars, or do you want to trade it in as a part-exchange?
- Do you have strong feelings about the manufacturer's country of origin?
- Is reliability a key issue?

● If you are buying second-hand, do you want to pay for an independent inspection?

● How important is resale price?

You need to get into a position where you can produce a shortlist of possible cars that you are interested in. Once you have the shortlist, you need to research those models in more detail using magazines, the Internet and talking to friends and colleagues. This will probably help you to order your shortlist in terms of an initial preference.

Using the Internet, advertisements and published used car guides, you then need to work out what is your target price for each of the models on your shortlist.

Most people will want to test drive the shortlist using new and used car dealers. You must decide if you think that you owe these dealers any obligation to seriously consider their offers, or whether you will avail yourself of their service and then ruthlessly pursue the cheapest price (e.g. over the Internet). Alternatively, you may feel happy to repay a dealer by getting your new car serviced by them (they make much more profit from servicing than they do from car sales).

You also need to decide whether you will take the attitude that once you have found something you like, at a price you think is very competitive and you can afford, you will do a deal. Alternatively, you may want to wait till you have tried all the cars on your shortlist.

You are then ready to visit car sellers to try to get the best price for something you like and can afford. If you are using dealers then it is worth researching, usually via your friends and colleagues, whether they have a reputation for providing good service.

brilliant tip

Always remember when doing any negotiation the danger of 'analysis paralysis'. Preparation is an investment where you invest your time to try to satisfy your desire to buy something appropriate to your needs at the best possible price. You can always do more research, but you must decide when you have done enough preparation to start haggling or bargaining.

The Sharing

If you are buying from a dealer then you will want to discuss what cars are available that may meet your needs. A good dealer may make suggestions you had not thought of. You should check what promotions and other inducements are available. It is a good idea to mention models from other manufacturers that you are interested in, because it increases your leverage. You will probably want to arrange a test drive before you get down to haggling, because if you don't like the car you may as well save your and the salesman's time. You need to be very upfront about the fact that price is a very important issue for you. If you have a car to trade in then it is worth testing the salesman's reaction to it – most salesmen will be honest about whether the trade-in is an attractive item for them to sell on; in fact, it is not uncommon for a salesman to tell a potential customer that they would do better to sell their old car privately. Unsurprisingly, clean and polished cars are more attractive than dirty ones.

If you like the car you have test driven then you will either get straight down to haggling, or you may decide to wait till you have driven all the cars on your shortlist. There is no right way to decide this, but if you enjoy buying cars you may decide to do lots of test drives first, whilst if you aren't very interested in cars you might decide to see if you can secure a good deal straight away. Even if you intend to test drive other cars, you may well want to get a ballpark figure to change your car from the salesman before you leave.

Haggling

Screwing a good deal out of a car salesman is one of the most enjoyable negotiating situations. Flip through the *Haggling* chapter and use as many of the techniques as you like. Unless you have to make a purchase rapidly because your old car isn't roadworthy, then be patient and be willing to walk away from a less than good deal. You may be willing to pay a little more for a new car than you can get from an Internet dealer, but the Internet price should strongly influence what you are willing to pay.

brilliant tip

Make sure you stress that the only figure you are interested in is the price to change your car.

Don't be afraid to play dealers off against each other – for the same model, or different models.

If you are negotiating to buy a car privately then don't make the mistake of denigrating their car. Say you like it, but you can afford to pay only £X, and then haggle to try to agree an acceptable price. If possible, have cash in your pocket that you can take out and show to them. Insist on them taking you out for a test run, and be very attentive to any problems you can hear and feel. If you aren't knowledgeable then have an independent inspection or take a knowledgeable friend.

brilliant tip

When arranging to see a private car, ask on the telephone: 'Is the car still for sale?' If the seller asks which car you mean, then they aren't a private seller but are instead some sort of dealer, and hence your chance of bagging a bargain is low.

brilliant tip

When buying privately, remember to do the obvious checks. How worn are the tyres? Does the owner have a whole sheaf of paperwork that shows mileages and other indications that the car has been cared for? Remember to do an HPI check (or equivalent).

Always go to the seller's home; if they aren't willing to let you see where they live, walk away. Remember that when buying privately the law is basically 'buyer beware' and you have almost no legal protection. If you take the risk of buying privately or through an auction (where you will have limited protection), make sure you pay a sufficiently low price to cover the extra risks.

Multi-party negotiations

I was tempted to open this example with the supposed inscription at the entrance to Hell:

Abandon hope all ye who enter here

The worst negotiating experience many experienced negotiators will have faced will have been in multi-party negotiations, especially if they involve cross-cultural and language barriers.

Abandon hope all ye who enter here

Having accepted that you are in for a long and painful experience is there anything that can be done to reduce the pain? There are three techniques that can help:

1 Ensure that the parties have an in-depth meta negotiation at the start. You must agree on how decisions are going to be taken. Is there going to be a strong lead partner in the negotiation whose word is law? Are you going to insist on decisions being taken by consensus, or will one or more dissenting voices be allowed? Is it going to be majority voting?

2 You need to agree rational processes. For example, in a consortium bid you may agree a standard method by which a partner calculates the charge-out rate for their staff. You may agree that the financial split in a consortium is based solely on work share. You may agree that work share is determined by giving work packages to the most qualified partner, as decided by the consortium leader. You may split

up work packages by drawing lots and then choosing in turn. Without rational processes you are in trouble!

3 You need to get each party to put their deal breakers on the table upfront. For example, if you have been told by your stakeholders that you must achieve a minimum work share, then you need to gain your partners' acceptance that they are willing to start negotiations knowing that you have such a constraint.

Final words

There really is no need to fear negotiations. Negotiations are a game, and you now understand the rules of the game and the tactics you can use to win a good deal. If you apply the lessons you have learnt you will immediately see the beneficial effects. As your confidence and experience build, the deals you do will get better and better. Even if you are not someone who currently enjoys the great game of negotiations, there is absolutely no reason why you cannot end up having fun as you get the best deals for yourself and your employer.

The lessons you have learnt have all been extensively 'tested in combat' – in my personal life, in dozens of large, set-piece commercial negotiations, and hundreds of situations where I represented trades union members. I was professionally trained and have read most of the best-selling negotiating books. My experience, training and studies have allowed me to extract simple principles, tactics and advice that can easily be applied in your personal and professional lives.

> set yourself a challenging target and then go for it

Set yourself a challenging target and then go for it. There is nothing wrong with wanting to walk away with the biggest slice of the cake that you can get away with; and there is no reason why you cannot have it whilst retaining the respect of your opponent. The world admires tough and skilful negotiators, and I very much hope I have helped you towards this goal.

If you follow the advice in this book you will be able to enjoy getting what you want … and maybe a little bit more!